WHAT'S GOING ON HERE?

WHAT'S GOING ON HERE?

The *Harper's Magazine*
Book of Annotations

Foreword by Lewis H. Lapham

Edited by Colin Harrison

Delta

A Delta Book
Published by
Dell Publishing
a division of
Bantam Doubleday Dell Publishing Group, Inc.
666 Fifth Avenue
New York, New York 10103

Library of Congress Cataloging in Publication Data

    What's going on here?: the Harper's Magazine book of annotations/ foreword by Lewis H. Lapham ; edited by Colin Harrison.
    p.   cm.
    ISBN 0-385-30400-5 (pbk.) : $10.00
    1. Harper's Magazine. 2. American wit and humor. 3. English Language—Terms and phrases—Humor.
    I. Harrison, Colin.   II. Harper's
    PN6162.W46 1991
    817'.5408—dc20   91-10842
                                         CIP

Manufactured in the United States of America
Published simultaneously in Canada

November 1991
10 9 8 7 6 5 4 3 2 1
K P P

ACKNOWLEDGMENTS

The diligent work of a number of people has made this book possible.

Many of the annotations in this collection were originally conceived and edited by Gerald Marzorati, senior editor at *Harper's Magazine*. Debra Rust, art director at *Harper's*, solved various difficulties in reproducing documents, and assistant editor Elliott Rabin fact-checked all copy for accuracy. Editorial reaction and guidance came from the entire editorial staff, including Lewis Lapham, Michael Pollan, Ellen Rosenbush, Jack Hitt, Ilena Silverman, Charis Conn, and Paul Tough. Among former editors at the magazine, Robert Karl Manoff, Janet Gold, Mark Danner, Pam Abrams, and Eric Etheridge should also be recognized. Jeanne Dubi and Frank DiBartolo managed the business aspects of the book.

My thanks go also to Emily Reichert at Delacorte Press, who put in endless hours discussing the concept and execution of the book and whose enthusiasm and organization carried the project forward. I'm also indebted to Jenny Delson at Delacorte, who got the book started there, and to Kevin Doherty, who assisted in the book's production.

C.H.

CONTENTS

FOREWORD

Eight years ago this coming spring *Harper's Magazine* revised its editorial method and design to conform to the spirit of an age grown impatient with what used to be known as the news. The accelerating speeds of the mass media have accustomed the modern reader to the techniques of film, to shorter texts and longer lists, to a preference for metaphors and the juxtapositions of images as distant from one another as Madonna and Mrs. George Bush. If the magazine wished to hold its audience, it had no choice but to change with the times and redraft its purposes in ways that matched the forms of perception familiar to the late twentieth century.

The problem was the surfeit of information. Besieged with data of every conceivable denomination, everybody had access every week to so much news and entertainment that hardly anybody could follow the plot or hum the tune. More turned out to be less, and what was wanted were the means of resolving the blurred images into some sort of plausible focus. The media hold up so many mirrors at so many angles to the society that nothing can be safely boxed off, not even by an enterprising journalist with a talent for adjectives or extortion.

Nor can the mass media be counted upon for interpretation. They offer for sale every conceivable fact or opinion, and their collective enterprise bears comparison to that of the British raiding units in North Africa during World War II pressing far behind the German lines in search of stray pieces of metal. The patrols collected anything that came to hand—a shell casing, a broken axle, a button torn from the uniform of a dead corporal. The objects were sent to Cairo for analysis, and by this means British Intelligence guessed at the condition of the German war machine.

Given the modern barrage of incoming information, it is no longer a matter of discovering the secret that nobody knows (the identity of Deep Throat, the causes of the war with Iraq, the whereabouts of Jimmy Hoffa's corpse), but rather it is a matter of locating the obvious within an intelligible sequence or context.

In the natural sciences the problem had been apparent for some years, and the physicists and biologists had learned to imagine the complex lines of causation running through an atom or an estuary. As long ago as 1975 it was common-place to say that we live in an interdependent world, but relatively few people in the media trades took the phrase as anything other than a pompous syn-onym for confusion. But the complex lines of causation also run through the cultural and political provinces of experience, binding together the economies of nations and unified fields of human thought. If the lines become hard to see in a world more accurately represented by the randomness of quantum mechanics than by Newton's geometry, then they can be brought into view only by acts of the imagination.

It was with this hope in mind that the editors of *Harper's Magazine* introduced an anthology of new forms, among them the "Index," the "Forum," the "Readings," and the "Annotation." Under each heading the emphasis falls on the specific instance rather than the general statement, and the intention is diagnostic, not therapeutic. The magazine favors the bias of the humanities and relies on the unashamedly partial evidence available to the investigative scientist and the observant novelist. Flaubert could think of no endeavor more ennobling than the contemplation of reality, and the late I. I. Rabi, the Nobel prize–winning physicist at Columbia University, conceded a similar preference when he said that physics (by which he meant the basic structure of reality) was "the only study proper to a gentleman." Writers as distant from one another in time as the younger Pliny and Walker Percy sought to know the world as it is, not as it is more or less immaculately conceived in the canons of political doctrine and ethical romance.

Among all of the magazine's various attempts at gentlemanly study, the one that delights me the most is the "Annotation." Perhaps this is because I once intended to become an historian, and the annotation is an historian's device signed to a contemporary document. Or maybe it is because I like crossword puzzles and detective stories. So many of the documents with which I find myself confronted (not only printed forms but also photographs and commercial advertisements, airplane tickets, as well as bank statements, government licenses, and letters of introduction) seem to me as difficult to decipher as the runes drawn by an old and wandering druid. When I get the thing right—why this rule or that exception, why so pale a color blue behind the woman in the bath, et cetera—I feel that I have just managed to understand something important told to me by a Turkish customs official on the Armenian frontier.

None of us escapes the tyranny of paper, and the "Annotation" published nearly every month in *Harper's Magazine* is meant to arm the reader with the means of self-defense. Our lives and fortunes depend on documents of all kinds and descriptions, documents that most of us sign without thinking and seldom bother to read beyond the first sentence.

In the effort to render the modern world more intelligible (if not necessarily more beautiful or kind), the editors assign the documents to individuals capable of explicating the text—the hospital bill to a physician, the trial transcript to a lawyer, the college application to a university president. The object is not to make easy jokes about the fatuity of this or that bureaucracy but rather to make clear the meaning of the language too often used like paint, to conceal the plaster of the thought.

As with every other text published in *Harper's Magazine*, the device of the "Annotation" assumes the complicity of a reader willing to draw his or her own conclusions. Unlike some of the more gilded mirrors of the media, the magazine doesn't present a reflection of a society that looks just the way everybody always wanted it to look. Nor does the magazine presume to tell people what to say about the season's newest book, how to behave in the presence of money, what thoughts to think while drinking chilled white wine on the beach at Acapulco, what moral attitude to adopt in a discussion about abortion or the hydrogen bomb. Some readers apparently welcome this sort of thing, and they expect their magazines to clothe them with opinions in the way that Ralph Lauren or Bloomingdale's dresses them for the opera. The readers of *Harper's*, I suspect, always belonged to a different crowd. They strike me as the kind of people who would rather have the tools to work the American grain into a knowledge of their own making.

— Lewis H. Lapham
Editor,
Harper's Magazine

INTRODUCTION

Modern life is a life of paper. From the moment of birth until well after death we knowingly and unknowingly generate and elicit a blizzard of documentation that chases our lives: birth records, doctors' bills, immunization histories, school transcripts, employment files, phone bills, canceled checks, apartment leases, psychological evaluations, medical records, letters, resumes, merchandise order forms, airplane, train, and bus tickets, living wills, gun registration forms, theater tickets, passports, bank statements, driver's licenses, census forms, paychecks, state and federal tax records, surrogate parenting contracts, divorce agreements, prison records, credit histories, mortgage papers, organ-donor agreements, wills, death certificates, autopsy reports, and so on—the list is endless.

Yet the grist that you or I generate is meager compared to the avalanche spilling forth from corporations, institutions, and the government. Again, a partial list: official forms, regulations, employee records, press releases, minutes of public proceedings, congressional reports and records, advertising, warranties, public-service messages, secret files, lists of officials, junk mail in its infinite variety, budget projections, revenue reports, cost-overrun memos, lists of ingredients, transcripts of murder trials, owner's manuals, trademark filings, product recall notifications, form letters, junk faxes, summonses, sales projections, memoranda, stocks, bonds, pamphlets, fliers, newspapers, magazines, books, position papers, litigation depositions, class-action suits, corporate loan agreements, and so on.

Clearly, we are to be congratulated. Somehow in the course of life, we more or less negotiate our way through all this stuff, through the endless information and noninformation and record-keeping and sensory overload. To survive mentally we give most of the paper swirling about us only a cursory look—and therein is a dilemma and the moment of this book. Some paper is extraordinarily important: our personal lives may turn on a document hastily signed, our nation's life can quietly be changed by the obscure law or regulation slipped onto the government's books. When do we have the time to examine such papers with care? What if we don't know what we're looking at? And what do we look for?

The word *document* comes through the Middle English and Old French from the Latin *documentum:* lesson, example, warning; from *docére,* to teach. The editors of *Harper's Magazine* have taken it as truth that documents can teach and warn us, if only we bring to them certain information. Eight years ago, working from Lewis Lapham's vision for a new magazine, editors Robert Karl Manoff and Gerald Marzorati tested and refined the journalistic form of the annotation. A regular section of the magazine is now given over to the reproduction of a document on a two-page spread with an opinionated, factual commentary pointing to specific elements of the document. At *Harper's,* we call this section the "Annotation." By annotating different elements of the document, we seek to explain it. But more than just explain it. We seek to debunk, to contextualize, to deconstruct, to unveil what appears to be simple or innocuous or straightforward, and get at the more complicated reality behind it.

Many of the documents reproduced in this book were not meant for public inspection. Their very unpreparedness is satisfyingly authentic; signatures are scrawled, the typing is crooked, information is communicated in jargon or shorthand, lines have been crossed out, and the document has been carelessly stamped with various bureaucratic imprimaturs. The visual texture of such a document suggests that no one expects it will be seen, that the secrets within will never be known. One of the best examples (see page 22) is Sharon Danann's August 1990 annotation of a computer-generated statistical evaluation of the workday of an airline reservationist. Despite being a clear harbinger of the dark side of America's postindustrial service economy, the document *appears* to be nothing more than columns of numbers printed out with a lousy dot-matrix printer. But scrawled on the sheet are the supervisor's angry warnings that the reservationist is not working hard enough, based on the numbers. Danann unpacks the computer's "percent utilization" judgment of the worker's day, and the numbers reveal a woman working terribly hard, handling seventy-nine calls in the day and hurrying her paperwork, all the while knowing that her supervisor may be eavesdropping on her performance.

In stark contrast are documents created in order to be read and inspected. The typing is perfect, the phraseology purposeful. Here we may detect the oily euphemism, the oblique jargonizing of common English and the Latinate presentation of official lies. See Alexander Cockburn and Ken Silverstein's September 1988 annotation on page 52 of a letter from the then–secretary of the navy, John Lehman, to Congressman Denny Smith (R.-Ore.). Lehman's letter is a response to Smith's questioning of the technical accuracy of the Navy's AEGIS radar system, and is full of phrases such as "the most carefully tested combat system ever built," "extensive operational testing," "have proven successful," and "affirms our full confidence." It is meant to rationalize the choice and cost of the radar system, which costs about $500 million per unit, according to the authors. The AEGIS, as they point out, is the same radar system used on the cruiser USS *Vincennes* and which misidentified Iran Air Flight 655, the Airbus aircraft that the *Vincennes* shot down, killing 290 men, women, and children.

The annotations in this book date from 1984 to the present. Some, such as the U.S. Standard Certificate of Death, annotated by Michael Zimecki (see page 96), have changed little over time. On it we may see the exact line which, when filled out in the obligatory indelible ink, is used to calculate national death rates. It is, writes Zimecki, "our last offering to a bureaucracy that reduces lives to numbers." Other annotations in these pages found their origin at specific moments in our recent collective history. In March of 1985, shortly after Ronald Reagan began his second term, and with the real estate and stock markets floating to ever more precipitous heights, restaurants around the country boomed as people put their easily gained dollars into their mouths and not into savings. That month, *Harper's* ran an annotation of the menu from Le Cirque, one of New York's most status conscious restaurants (see page 26). Written by Mimi Sheraton, former food critic at *Time*, the annotation explains that Nancy Reagan preferred the lobster salad (then $20.75) at Le Cirque, and that the management gladly sent it to her while she was at her hairdresser's salon not far away. The First Lady, of course, was merely one illustrious personage among many at Le Cirque; sitting beneath "murals of monkeys dressed as humans and aping social situations" were Richard Nixon, Dustin Hoffman, Nancy Kissinger, Roy Cohn, et cetera. Sheraton reminds us, with a quick wink, that the monkeys were not intended "as commentary on [the] preening, chattering guests."

While it is a delight to mock the ephemeral (who cares *now* what kind of salad Nancy Reagan prefers?), it is also necessary to mark the enduring changes in society, especially changes driven by advancing technology that deliver us into morally complex dilemmas. These, too, have their moment—after which there is often no going back. And what better example but the now famous surrogate parenting agreement between Mary Beth Whitehead and William and Elizabeth Stern? In April of 1987 the first page of their legal contract to make a baby by artificial insemination appeared in *Harper's*, annotated by Judith Levine (see page 40). Levine identifies the potential for "creepy" class exploitation in surrogate mothering (the Sterns's 1987 income of $90,000 was more than three times that of Mary Beth Whitehead and her husband, Richard) and reports that the wage the two parties agreed on was about $1.50 an hour. "Surrogate mothering," writes Levine, "like pornography, is situated in that volatile zone where law and ethics, commerce and the body, intersect and widely divergent moralities collide. Lawmakers and judges cannot possibly foresee every problem. Yet they must begin to make some binding decisions. Families—especially children—can no longer afford to wait."

So it is that documents, once under examination, spur us to ask questions. How does the application for a Swiss bank account convey secrecy? In a typical news photo, what does mobster John Gotti's stonelike hair tell us about how he intimidates members of the jury? Looking at the written symbols for the dance steps of Balanchine's *Nutcracker*, can we perceive the almost impossible grace required? How was it that Patrick Purdy—the man who killed five children and wounded twenty-nine more in a Stockton, California, elementary school—possessed a record of criminal charges and yet successfully filled out a federal gun form when buying the AK-47 rifle he used in the mass murder? How does a professional food photographer trick up the meal to make it look so impossibly appetizing? How do the national television networks conduct their secret polls on election night? The answers are revealed in the documents in this book.

America of the 1990s is a tricky place. We should be dubious of the received wisdom of the media pundits, of politicians, of the vision of reality presented to us by credit card commercials, of the prefabricated appetites we are conditioned to feel. We had best look more closely at what is around us, especially at documents that seem utterly clear or that overtly purport to tell us who we are. The annotated documents that follow are a good place to begin. They indicate the subversive complexity of our culture and politics. Again, they teach and they warn.

— Colin Harrison
Associate Editor,
Harper's Magazine

WHAT'S GOING ON HERE?

For most of human history, births have been recorded only by those whose lives they touched. The modern state, however, has other needs. Mercantilist economic theories foresaw material benefits accruing from large populations; to monitor growth, Sweden began keeping birth records in the seventeenth century through its official churches. For public-health reasons, Britain implemented a reporting system in the 1830s. Georgia became the first of the states to require birth certificates, in 1823; New York City followed suit in 1847. Until 1866, when the first version of this form was designed for use, births were entered in ledgers kept by the city. But reporting of births was sporadic until 1874, when New York promulgated rules for doing so, complete with a schedule of fees for such things as records, searches, and copies (the birth was registered free—and still is).

The presumption here is that babies are born in hospitals—and today, in the United States, most babies are. It was not always so. Women in colonial America followed the British practice of "lying in," having their babies at home in a feminine ritual overseen by a midwife and shared by the mother's neighbors and kin. Beginning in the late eighteenth century, as industrialization and urbanization loosened local social bonds, and as the birth process became more technical, men increasingly replaced women at the bedside. Birthing itself was to become an institutional event: by 1970 over 99 percent of the country's babies were opening their eyes to delivery-room lights. It is easy to forget how recently all of this happened: the medical profession had no nationwide standards for obstetrical practice until 1930, and as recently as 1940 only 56 percent of all births were taking place in hospitals.

Joan Daley is about six years older than the typical first-time American mother, whose age has risen slightly over the past two decades (to 23.3 years in 1983). Daley is one of many women who are pursuing careers before having children—and then having fewer of them. Women between the ages of thirty and thirty-four are more than twice as likely to give birth for the first time as they were a decade ago. But the fertility rate for the childbearing population as a whole has dropped to 1.8 children per woman (compared with six in 1780). Every year the childbearing generation in America is coming up about 600,000 babies short of reproducing itself.

Robert Karl Manoff was managing editor of Harper's Magazine *from 1983 to 1985 and is now director of the Center for War, Peace, and the News Media at New York University.*

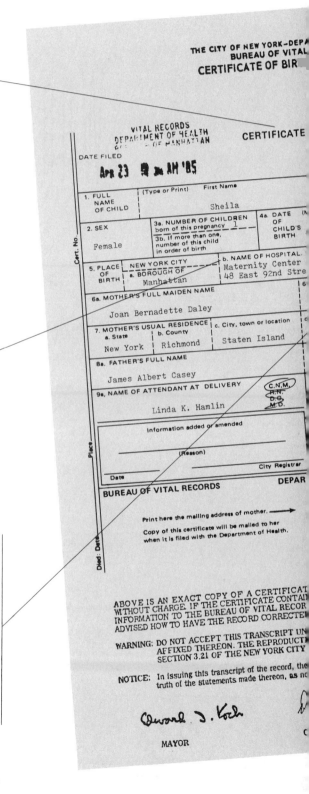

A NATION

es, by Robert Karl Manoff

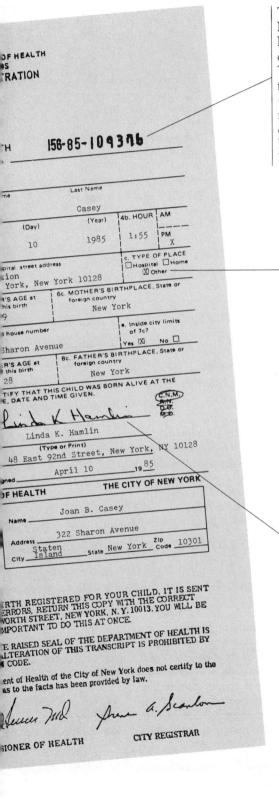

OF HEALTH
RATION

156-85-109376

	Last Name		
	Casey		
(Day)	(Year)	4b. HOUR	AM
10	1985	1:55	PM X

c. TYPE OF PLACE
☐ Hospital ☐ Home
☒ Other

York, New York 10128

6c. MOTHER'S BIRTHPLACE, State or foreign country
New York

e. Inside city limits of 7c?
Yes ☒   No ☐

Sharon Avenue

8c. FATHER'S BIRTHPLACE, State or foreign country
New York

TIFY THAT THIS CHILD WAS BORN ALIVE AT THE
, DATE AND TIME GIVEN.

C.N.M.

Linda K. Hamlin

Linda K. Hamlin
(Type or Print)
48 East 92nd Street, New York, NY 10128

April 10   19 85

THE CITY OF NEW YORK

Name   Joan B. Casey

Address   322 Sharon Avenue

City Staten Island   State New York   Zip Code 10301

RTH REGISTERED FOR YOUR CHILD. IT IS SENT
RRORS, RETURN THIS COPY WITH THE CORRECT
ORTH STREET, NEW YORK. N.Y. 10013. YOU WILL BE
MPORTANT TO DO THIS AT ONCE.

E RAISED SEAL OF THE DEPARTMENT OF HEALTH IS
LTERATION OF THIS TRANSCRIPT IS PROHIBITED BY
CODE.

ent of Health of the City of New York does not certify to the
as to the facts has been provided by law.

SIONER OF HEALTH   CITY REGISTRAR

The first three digits (156) are the code assigned to New York City under the Uniform System for the Numbering of Birth Certificates. The following two digits (85) refer to the year the birth was registered. The number to the right of the second dash (1) identifies the borough of the city where the birth took place (Manhattan); and the last five digits (09376), the number of this birth for the particular year and borough. Sheila Casey was one of over 3.7 million babies born in the United States in 1985, and one of 302 born in New York City on this day.

In New York the only sanctioned "other" place of birth available is the Childbearing Center, run out of an East Side townhouse by the Maternity Center Association. Established in 1975 as an alternative to highly technological—which can mean impersonal—in-hospital care, the center is one of some 130 independent birth facilities in the country. Each year, between 15,000 and 20,000 women have their babies at such centers. The MCA record is impressive: because the center admits only women with low-risk pregnancies and then discourages unnecessary technological intervention, fewer than 6 percent of center mothers undergo Caesarean sections, compared with a national average of 20.3 percent (up from 5.5 percent in 1970). Moreover, no center mother has found it necessary to name MCA as the primary respondent in a malpractice suit; over 70 percent of this country's obstetricians have been sued by their patients.

A nurse-midwife trained at Columbia University and certified by the American College of Nurse Midwives, Linda K. Hamlin has delivered more than 400 babies in the eighteen years she has been practicing. Although she has never been sued—only 6 percent of the 2,500 active nurse-midwives in the country have been—the profession nevertheless is being caught up in the national crisis created by malpractice litigation. This year insurance to cover its seven midwives is costing the center $965. If the New York State Insurance Department approves the proposals now before it, however, the premium will rise to $430,185. But despite such prospects, midwifery is regaining legitimacy. Increasing numbers of hospitals have instituted their own birthing units, and midwives are once again assuming a role in attending the scores of thousands of home births that still take place. Meanwhile, it is useful to keep the struggle for control over American childbearing in perspective: according to the World Health Organization, 45 percent of all women who give birth in the world today continue to do so with no trained medical help whatsoever.

WOOD, THA'

Getting a grip on the Louisv

While an epidemic of greed kept the baseball season at bay this spring, back in Louisville, Kentucky, Hillerich & Bradsby, purveyor to the national pastime, was stockpiling supplies for the millionaires of summer. A ballplayer's most precious instrument—other than his paycheck—is his bat, and roughly 70 percent of the pros take a Louisville Slugger to the plate. (The rest of the pro market is split between the Rawlings, Cooper, and Worth brands.) Long part of the baseball iconography, the Louisville Slugger trade name is recognized by nine out of ten Americans. The Slugger originated more than a century ago when Pete Browning, star of the Louisville Eclipse, broke his bat and seventeen-year-old John "Bud" Hillerich turned a replacement on the lathe in his father's woodworking shop. Browning used Hillerich's bat in his next game and went three for three. The bat's mystique established, orders from Browning's teammates and other ballplayers soon followed. The sentimental aura of the Slugger, however, like virtually every other aspect of the game, serves a $1.15 billion engine of commerce.

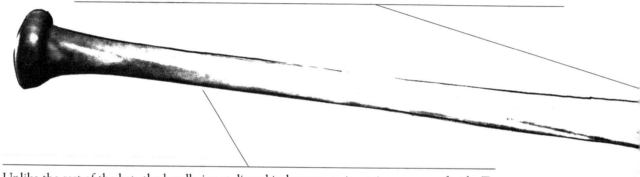

Unlike the rest of the bat, the handle is not dipped in lacquer, so it retains a coarser finish. To enhance the grip, players may use cork, tape, rosin, pine tar, or dirt on the handle. All other substances are banned. Only amateur bats have their length stamped on the knob. Only pros can dictate their handle dimensions and what kind of knob they want at the end of the bat. A few opt for a "cone-knobbed" bat, which tapers off without a knob at the end. The lack of a knob enables the batter—primarily one who likes to bunt—to dump the bat quickly on the way to first base. It's a slight edge. Even a few extra hits here and there over a season make a difference and count for thousands of dollars come time for contract negotiations.

Six different grades of timber are used in the Louisville Slugger, of which "125" is the highest professional grade. Almost all of the bats are turned from northern white ash from New York and Pennsylvania, though a small percentage are made of maple or hackberry. The trees must be at least sixty years old before they are cut, and their wood must be seasoned for up to six months before being turned on the Louisville lathes. Each tree trunk provides roughly sixty bats. In an average season, major and minor league teams purchase about seven dozen bats per player—a total of about 180,000—for from fifteen to eighteen dollars each, slightly below cost. H&B, still controlled by the Hillerich family of Louisville, sells the bats at a loss because the Slugger name boosts sales of the company's other products—aluminum bats, golf clubs, assorted baseball equipment—which, with the pro bats, total $70 million per year.

Francis Wilkinson is a writer living in New York City.

IT BE TRUE
Slugger, *by Francis Wilkinson*

In 1905 Honus Wagner became the first big leaguer to have his signature on a bat, thus blazing the product-endorsement trail that has enriched athletes from Johnny Unitas to Michael Jordan. Since then, H&B has entered into signature contracts with 6,000 players; during any one season, nine out of ten major league players have a signature contract with a bat manufacturer. H&B markets a dozen signature bats each year, balancing the choice of names according to race, geography, and league. Of course, only the signatures of star players make it to the sporting-goods store. Signature bats sold to the public have the same dimensions as bats used by their respective signatories, but the weight may vary. (Pro bats are meticulously selected and weighed to assure uniformity for each player.) H&B contracts, which sometimes outlast a player's career, are positively quaint by the norms of a game in which the average salary is $557,000 a year. When a player signs with H&B he chooses a payment of $300 or a set of golf clubs. Just as big-league scouts look for talent, H&B watches for tomorrow's stars, signing promising minor league players while they're still green enough to succumb to flattery and a set of golf clubs. H&B spotted Pete Rose when he was in the minors and wisely offered him a contract. Toward the end of Rose's career, however, perhaps as his gambling debts accrued, he ended his agreement with H&B and signed a lucrative, exclusive contract to use the baseball products of the giant Japanese sporting goods firm Mizuno. In hindsight, H&B seems to have been the victim of good timing. It got an out-of-court settlement. And it got rid of Rose before he fell from grace.

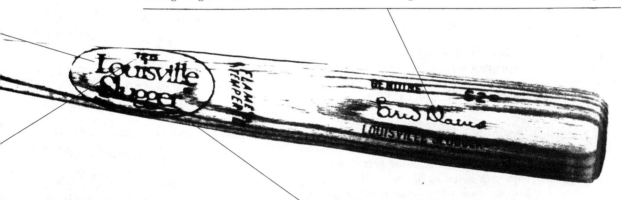

Under major league rules, the trademarked brand is restricted to one four-inch-long zone beginning eighteen inches from the end of the bat. In the 1989 World Series, while millions watched on television, Rickey Henderson used a black bat with LOUISVILLE spelled out in large white letters. Major League Baseball promises a crackdown. The brand is burned onto the bat at a 90-degree angle to the grain, the strongest part of the timber. That's why batters are told to keep the brand facing up when at the plate. But bats inevitably break. Babe Ruth once hit twenty-one home runs with a single bat before it splintered launching the twenty-first. When bats don't break, they sometimes plumb wear out. George Brett used the same bat through a thirty-game hitting streak in 1981. When the streak ended he returned the bat, explaining, "This bat has no more hits in it." Aluminum bats, on the other hand, never break and seem to have endless hits in them. Major League Baseball, mindful of the aesthetics of the grand old game, has so far rejected the powerful allure of the lighter aluminum, which dominates the amateur bat market. Aluminum bats, permitted in college play, result in higher scores and some team batting averages over .300. Baseball experts calculate that many stadiums are not large enough to contain the blasts that would ensue from an aluminum bat in the hands of, say, Eric Davis. But it's far from certain that wood will remain a protected species in the majors. Fans, played for suckers for years, may come to demand more home-plate fireworks for their billions.

A commission established by President Reagan to study ways to wipe out organized crime recently issued a 1,000-page report—and on page 452 called for widespread drug testing of Americans by their employers. As the President weighs this recommendation, he should bear in mind that urinalysis, the most common means of testing, gives an organization a window into the private lives of its employees—and power to demand loyalty, power even to punish dissent. He might also bear in mind the case of Leslie Price, thirty-three, and Susan Register, thirty-two, two former employees of Georgia Power—two of the 4.5 million workers tested last year.

The private sector hardly needs the nudge. Businesses have been supporting drug testing in rapidly growing numbers: 25 percent of Fortune 500 companies, for example, now do some form of testing. The firms have been spurred on by studies showing huge productivity losses as a result of drug use ($33.3 billion in 1983). Georgia Power was worried about productivity. It was more than $6 billion above its original estimates for construction costs and years behind schedule on its Plant Vogtle nuclear plant, where Price and Register worked.

In late 1984—with help from the paladin of testing, Peter B. Bensinger—Georgia Power implemented a drug-testing program at Plant Vogtle. Workers chosen at random would be given urine tests and a special hotline would be set up—a recorded message followed by three minutes of blank tape on which employees could finger co-workers. (Give dates and places, a woman's voice says.) One Georgia Power engineer wrote to an Augusta paper to say that while he was worried about safety and the role drugs play in undermining it, he thought the program was a "paranoid overreaction." Register, a $10.50-an-hour mechanical expediter, and Price, a $13.33-an-hour quality control inspector, were concerned about plant safety, too—they had reported apparent violations to the Nuclear Regulatory Commission. In early 1985, the two were told they'd been "hotlined," and were ordered in for tests.

Philip Weiss is a writer living in New York and a contributing editor at Harper's Magazine.

452

State failing this requirement.
electronic surveillance measure
with the proceeds thereof direc
constitute per se failure.

3. The President should dire
agencies to formulate immediat
implementing guidelines, inclu
programs, expressing the utter
Federal employees. State and l
the private sector should sup
that any and all use of drugs
contracts should not be award
implement drug programs, incl
Federal, State, or local gove
indirectly to programs that
condone illicit drug use in
which "decriminalized" the p
form of such condonation, an

4. States that have not
enforce laws prohibiting th

5. The states should be
about their prevention and
Institute on Drug Abuse. W
obtained from private prog

RINE TROUBLE

buses, *by Philip Weiss*

re to enact State

asset forfeiture provisions,

anti-drug programs, should

e heads of all Federal

lear policy statements, with

suitable drug testing

ceptability of drug abuse by

governments and leaders in

unequivocally a similar policy

nacceptable. Government

companies that fail to

suitable drug testing. No

t funds should go directly or

el "responsible" drug use or

ay. Laws in certain States

ssion of marijuana constitute a

uld be reconsidered.

dy done so should enact and

e of drug paraphernalia.

ired to report information

tment programs to the National

his information, and reports

NIDA will be better able to

What exactly is "suitable"? Georgia Power gave Price and Register the test most favored these days: the Emit st. The Emit st was brought on the market in 1981 by the Syva Company, which had received federal funding to come up with a cheap way to test for marijuana use. A company nurse, with the briefest training from Syva, can administer the Emit st and interpret the readouts ninety seconds later. And each test costs as little as $5, less than a tenth of more precise lab procedures. One problem: the st unit may give false positives for pot up to a third of the time.

Anyone who lives near a nuclear plant would agree that it's unacceptable for workers to be high. But there exist less intrusive ways of checking, such as hand-eye coordination tests. Susan Register wasn't so lucky. Suitable drug testing meant being forced by a nurse to drop her pants to her ankles, bend over at the waist with her knees slightly bent, hold her right arm in the air, and with her left hand angle a specimen bottle between her legs. She sobbed and shook, wet herself, and vomited. She was fired for insubordination: refusal to take another test. Price, meanwhile, was told her sample was positive for marijuana, and then fired for misconduct. Had she had been fired for drug use, the NRC might have suggested that the company recheck (at great cost) the work she had inspected as a quality controller.

Laws protecting whistleblowers are a source of comfort to Register and Price—they're suing for back pay and their jobs. Other laws now being considered across the country are no comfort at all. Republican legislators in Erie County, New York, recently introduced a bill that, if passed, would force all welfare recipients to undergo drug testing; the reasoning is they would become better candidates for employment (the implication is they're spending government money on dope). And a New Jersey high school wants permission to test its 500 students every September. The school superintendent explained that he wanted to make sure the kids were educated "in a healthful, safe, and loving atmosphere."

AND NOW, FOR SOMETH

What's coming up and goi

Twenty years ago this month, the architects of the Great Society set out to open a channel of high-minded communication free from commercial TV's wanton toadying to money. The founders pulled together a loose confederation of local educational and university stations and begot Public Television. The new medium promised new voices, more culture, and creative programming: quality television. Although eloquent about their purpose, the founders, alas, failed to establish a secure source of money. Instead of liberating PBS from the thrall of commerce, they shackled their good intentions to a Catherine wheel of perpetual need. As a result, this prime-time anniversary lineup is no cause for rejoicing. It is not so new and creative as it is cheap.

Shows of such unrelieved niceness as *Nature* and its multitudinous cousins are basement bargains. Some of *Nature*'s programs, for example, consist of canned footage purchased abroad at little cost. PBS finds an American host, shoots a few stand-ups, and tapes a whispery voice-over. Since animals don't speak in Japanese or Italian or German, the audience assumes the productions are new.

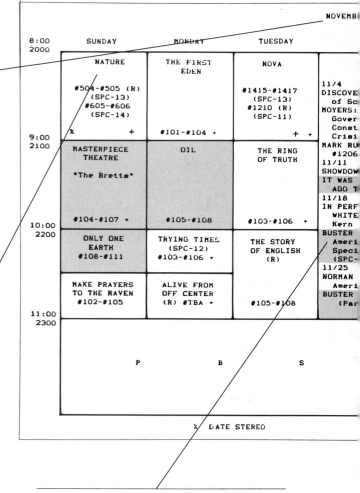

Foreign imports (shaded in gray) make up an astounding thirty-one of the eighty-four hours—more than a third—of this schedule. Importing a show costs a fraction of what it does to produce one. What PBS imports is often embarrassing. *Buster Keaton: An American Masters Special* is produced by Thames Television. Another upcoming series, *Television*—the history of a chiefly American phenomenon—is a re-edited British production. There is a reason for this: England spends about $30 per capita on public television while in America we spend less than a dollar.

Jack Hitt is a former senior editor at Harper's Magazine. *He is the editor of a dictionary of neologisms, and is at work on an account of a pilgrimage.*

IG COMPLETELY CHEAP

own at PBS, *by Jack Hitt*

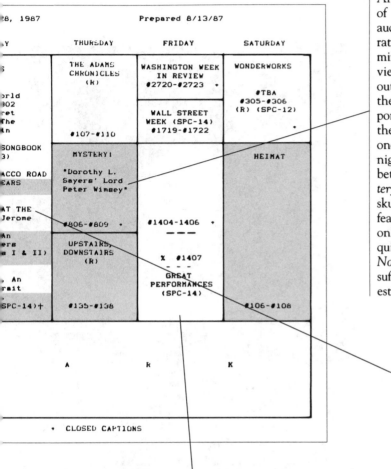

Another source of money is PBS's small crowd of viewers. Because only 10 percent of the audience contributes, PBS plays a Lilliputian ratings game. Like the networks, it sets programming to hold the audience—specifically, donor-viewers. This means building a mood throughout the evening or, in the jargon, "hooking them through the adjacencies." Notice the preponderance of hour-long shows, which reduces the dial-changing chances from two per hour to one. Also note the bland homogeneity of each night's offering: A truly original show wedged between Thursday's *The Adams Chronicles, Mystery!* and *Upstairs, Downstairs* would seem like a skunk at a lawn party. Other than furry animal features and Anglomaniacal soap operas, the only shows comfy in such fellowship are tranquilizing documentaries such as *The First Eden, Nova, The Story of English,* and *Discover,* which suffer from their only strength. They are interesting, very interesting, only interesting.

Even when PBS embarks on its own cultural programming, it relies on others. What C-SPAN does for Congress, PBS does for culture: It simply wheels its cameras into someone else's gig and rolls tape. Think of *In Performance at the White House, Live from Lincoln Center,* or a special broadcast direct from the Kennedy Center in Washington. To appreciate the keen pathos of what Public Television could be, consider the success of Public Radio. Despite similar problems, Public Radio established its own voice, created innovative programming, and launched such talents as Nina Totenberg, Bob Krulwich, and Garrison Keillor. In short, it created a network where there isn't one. PBS's voice is borrowed and its schedule patchwork.

Great Performances is made possible, as you know, by a grant from the Exxon Corporation. By untethering programmers from the constraints of product advertisement, PBS delivered itself into a more refined bondage: corporate sponsorship. Public Television could never produce a show that risks even so small a joke as *Max Headroom* because a company as stately as Exxon will not sponsor anything that lacks the pomp and majesty of heavy bronze. The occasional good idea for a program, then, is forced to beg. The producers of the acclaimed civil-rights history, *Eyes on the Prize,* suffered through a five-year pilgrimage to more than three dozen underwriters before making it on the air.

October 4, 1644, was the wedding day of Isabella Coymans, daughter of a rich textile manufacturer in the Dutch city of Haarlem, and Stephanus Geraerdts, a Haarlem alderman. These two paintings, each roughly four feet by three feet, were commissioned by Geraerdts six or seven years after the wedding. Love at First Sight (if that is what it was) has given way to a certain worldly wisdom: both partners have acquired the skills and gestures necessary for a conventional marriage in seventeenth-century Holland. The painter is Frans Hals, the first great modern portraitist. When he painted the Geraerdtses—more than a quarter of his portraits are of married couples—Hals was seventy, and at the height of his power as a sardonic observer. Nevertheless, Stephanus Geraerdts proudly hung the two paintings on either side of his fireplace.

In the paintings that recorded marriages in seventeenth-century Holland, the husband is always depicted slightly larger, slightly nearer to the spectator, as befits the owner presenting his spouse. The man is nearly always on the woman's right, the position of precedence (dexter). Paintings of the period were used somewhat as photographs might have been used, had photography existed. Painting had become independent of the royal courts and of the church; it had become a purely secular and domestic art. Paintings were done of families and of possessions. They were shown with pride to friends, and left to children. Above all they celebrated the values and mores of those who commissioned them.

Note Geraerdts's gold brocade and his wife's pearls. Both husband and wife were from families that belonged to Holland's new merchant class, the Holland of the Dutch East India Company, the richest country in Europe. On the wall behind them we see the family crests, by which the sitters, like all *nouveaux riches* of the time, set great store. The family name Coymans was derived from the Dutch word for cow. Many generations before.

A MARRIAGE

...ndscape, by John Berger

As Isabella and Stephanus look at each other—as they together pretend to be innocent of *our* looking at them—there is complicity. In her expression there is the calculation of her charm, a confidence in her desirability (for at least a few more years), an insincerity (she will tell the truth only when giggling or drunk), and yet—and this is what makes her unforgettable—a prudent but unrelenting mockery: she knows his weaknesses. In his expression there is calculation of a different kind. There is self-satisfaction—he has made a good marriage—and lechery. What is lacking in both faces is even a suspicion of love.

Isabella is dressed as if she has just come from her boudoir, Stephanus as if he has just returned from (or is heading for) the Exchange or the street. His place is the world, hers the home. Both are dressed in the very height of fashion, to the point of being slightly outrageous. He is overdressed: there is a little too much fine fabric. She is underdressed: her décolletage would have been a trifle "naughty" in her class and her time. Stephanus keeps one glove on. Isabella has a bow on her hip—the ribbon round the present—that whispers *undoing*. Perhaps his ungloved hand *will* undo it. More likely, Stephanus will leave the house without taking off his cape, and visit his favorite prostitute.

With her right hand Isabella offers her husband a rose. She holds the flower gently, pliantly, and thus at the same time she offers him her hand. The cuff of her right sleeve, unlike that of the left, is undone; we (and he) can see her arm disappearing tantalizingly into her dress. Stephanus holds out his right hand to receive his wife's offering. His cuff is buttoned, his gesture swift and formal. It is as though he were about to take from someone a legal document or a wad of money. Their hands combine through their gestures to say "dowry"—and everything that implies.

John Berger is the author, most recently, of Lilac and Flag *(Pantheon), the final volume of a fictional trilogy. The complete trilogy has just been published by Vintage.*

PIX FIX I

Accounting at Hollywood studios c

The *Trouble in Paradise* Lawsuit: In November 1988 writer Art Buchwald and producer Alain Bernheim sued Paramount Pictures for breach of contract, arguing that the Eddie Murphy vehicle *Coming to America*—the second highest-grossing film that year—was based on a story by Buchwald that Paramount had originally contracted Bernheim to produce. The Los Angeles Superior Court agreed, and ruled that Paramount must pay Buchwald and Bernheim their due share. The response from Paramount? The studio claims it *lost money* on the film, so no "net participation" profits were forthcoming. Now, in a new phase of the litigation likely to commence this winter, the court will examine Paramount's books—it could be the first time a major studio will stand trial for its accounting practices. Table I, from the sworn declaration of Carmen Desiderio, a Paramount VP for contract accounting, purports to demonstrate just how *Coming to America* managed to "lose" money; what the table and Desiderio's calculations would seem to show is the accounting *Fantasia* of the business end of the movie business.

The *Outrageous Fortune Is Less Than Zero* Gambit: By December of 1989, *Coming to America* had grossed $320 million worldwide, including domestic box office ($129 million), foreign box office ($138 million), HBO, soundtrack, etc. Paramount claims the modest amount of $125.3 million as its share after the exhibitors and middlemen took their cuts. But, assert the plaintiffs, this figure includes only 20 percent of the $44.5 million Paramount collected from home video sales—the studio stashed the remaining $35.6 million in its own video subsidiary, out of reach of "net" participants. Moreover, Paramount so far has refused to provide details of its pay-television revenues. Could this mean millions of dollars more?

The *Welcome to L.A.*, *Show of Force* Tactic: The distribution fee is the amount the studio awards itself to maintain its own distribution arm, which oversees advertising, transportation of reels, etc. It's a percentage of the gross—nearly pure profit—and also the figure the studios use to withhold profits from the majority of "talent"—actors, writers, directors—who, enticed by a vision of "back end" riches, accept a "net participation" profit-sharing deal. The catch: After the studio subtracts the distribution fee, there is often no "net." However, a few Hollywood people are powerful enough to get the big easy: "gross participation"—a straight percentage of the gross receipts *before* the studio lops off its distribution fee. Who commands "true gross"? No one in Hollywood is certain of the complete list, but everyone loves to speculate: Murphy, Stallone, Nicholson, Cruise.

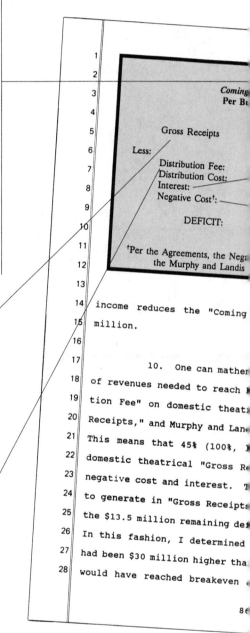

income reduces the "Coming
million.

10. One can mather
of revenues needed to reach
tion Fee" on domestic theatr
Receipts," and Murphy and Lan
This means that 45% (100%,
domestic theatrical "Gross R
negative cost and interest. 1
to generate in "Gross Receipt
the $13.5 million remaining de
In this fashion, I determined
had been $30 million higher tha
would have reached breakeven

D ADD?
n't square, divides, *by Leslie Brenner*

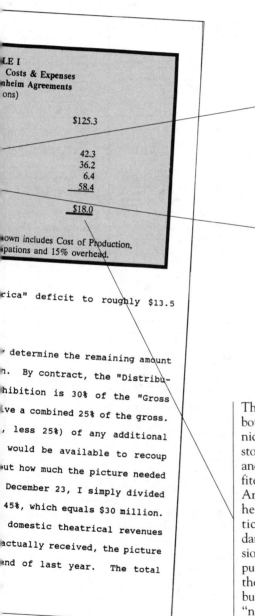

LE I
Costs & Expenses
nheim Agreements
ons)

$125.3

42.3
36.2
6.4
58.4

$18.0

own includes Cost of Production,
pations and 15% overhead.

cica" deficit to roughly $13.5

determine the remaining amount
n. By contract, the "Distribu-
hibition is 30% of the "Gross
ive a combined 25% of the gross.
, less 25%) of any additional
would be available to recoup
ut how much the picture needed
December 23, I simply divided
45%, which equals $30 million.
domestic theatrical revenues
actually received, the picture
end of last year. The total

The *High Anxiety, Risky Business* Swindle: Moviemaking is a perilous enterprise in which two out of three movies "lose" money, studio execs often weep, and so, being wise guys, they deduct from gross receipts the interest (125 percent of the prime rate) that their capital could have earned had it been parked in a CD rather than "gambled" on a movie. Furthermore, Paramount calculated some of this interest on monies eventually doled out to Murphy and director John Landis for their gross participations—funds that were not advanced as a cost of production but were paid out *after* gross receipts were in. Paramount also pays itself interest on the negative cost markups mentioned above. Thus Paramount pays itself over and over again, just for being Paramount, pockets more than $50 million, then calls the picture a loser.

The *Golden Child, Terms of Endearment* Padding Trick: This amount is the cost of developing and producing a negative from which prints are made. As the footnote indicates, the negative cost included direct production costs totaling a whopping $40 million. Not so, say the plaintiffs. Their research has Paramount marking up the cost of oil and gas 50 percent and lumber that is rechargeable to other productions 5 percent—and burying here $1 million in Eddie Murphy entourage expenses: limousines, bodyguards, mobile phones, VCRs, boom boxes, even $256 for one trip to McDonald's. Why should Paramount lavish such endless love on Murphy? Because Murphy's movies grossed $883 million for the studio from 1982 through 1988.

The *Easy Money, Gone With the Wind* Finale: Here's the bottom line "loss" figure. Never mind Paramount Communication Inc.'s own 1989 annual report, which brags to its stockholders that *Coming to America* had "strong domestic and international theatrical results" that significantly benefited "motion picture earnings for fiscal 1988." If the Los Angeles Superior Court agrees with Buchwald's and Bernheim's contentions about Paramount's accounting practices, the plaintiffs will win millions in compensatory damages. If the court finds clear evidence of "fraud, oppression or malice" by Paramount, the two may be entitled to punitive damages as well. But even more significant is that the major studios would be forced to change the way they do business—no longer would the usually empty promise of "net participation" suffice, and no longer would the major studios be allowed to justify their accounting practices on the grounds that talent agrees to them. Is this the turning point? Will the studios have to stand and deliver? Or will the court render them untouchables?

Leslie Brenner is a writer living in New York City.

POLITICS TAKEN

The census form: A partisar

Every ten years since 1790 the United States has enumerated itself, and on April 1 the country shall commence to do so once again. Census Bureau forms like this one, filled out by millions of Americans, tell us not only how many we are but also, and more important, *who* we are societally: what our racial and ethnic compositions are, where we live, and whether we are better off now than at the beginning of the previous decade. Census taking, then, is political: The information gathered is used for congressional redistricting, enforcement of the Voting Rights Act, and distribution of billions of dollars of federal grants-in-aid to states and localities. And the form itself is a product of political maneuvering. In what it has chosen to ask and what it has not, the Bush administration is counting on a count that will accent the positive and downplay the need for increased social spending.

The 1990 census will provide figures on how blacks fared during the Reagan-Bush years, but these numbers won't be complete. Blacks and Hispanics are the most undercounted populations, and middle-aged black males are undercounted by nearly 20 percent. The Census Bureau admits that the last census undercounted the population by 3.2 million people, half of whom were black. The undercount affects cities most; New York, for example, estimates that more than 450,000 citizens were missed, at a cost of at least $675 million in government grants-in-aid. The 1990 undercount will be at least as large as 1980's, but the Commerce Department announced it would not adjust the figure upward. Cities with large black Democratic populations—such as New York, Chicago, and Miami—are poised to help with the effort to count as many people as possible, but relief will not be swift. The war over the statistical correction promises to linger for years in the Commerce Department, now controlled by the Bush administration, and in the courts, remade by Reagan administration appointments.

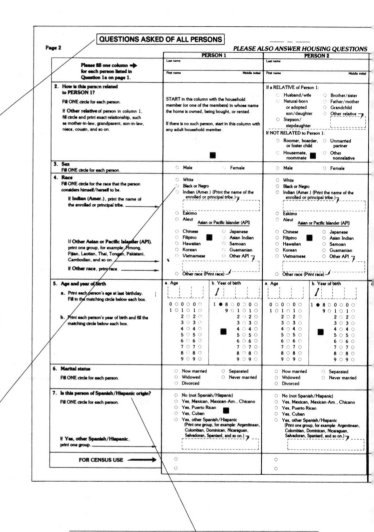

Hispanics—estimated at 20.1 million—are the fastest-growing segment of the population. Yet a Spanish-language form will not be sent to Hispanic households when the English forms are mailed. To receive Spanish forms, Hispanics—many of whom are undocumented aliens and don't read English—must call a number listed on the English form and ask for the Spanish one. Hispanic leaders requested years ago that Spanish-language forms be mailed to Hispanic neighborhoods. The Census Bureau says it costs too much.

Gwen Rubinstein is a graduate student at the University of Michigan School of Public Health.

INTO A COUNT

culation, *by Gwen Rubinstein*

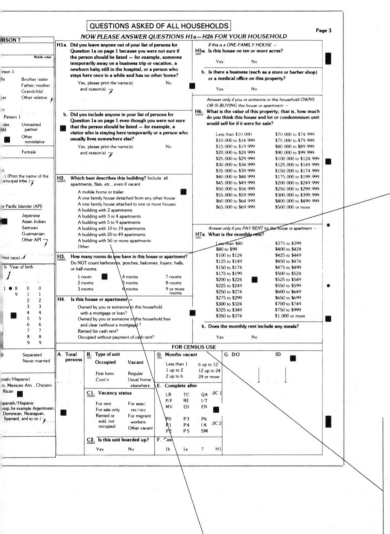

The president's Office of Management and Budget can reject or change federal paperwork. In its review of census materials, the OMB attempted to move questions H3, H5, H6, and H7 from this form, which goes to 88 million households, to the long form, which goes to only 17.7 million households. Question H3, long an important indicator of overcrowding, is crucially relevant: The 1980s saw American families having trouble finding decent, affordable housing while federal moneys for subsidized housing dropped dramatically and mortgage foreclosure rates climbed. Only by extraordinary public and congressional pressure was this question restored to this form. But the OMB succeeded in moving from the short form a standard question that asks if respondents have basic plumbing.

Presumably, the use of census information benefits all of us. But it is clear that in this era of budget constraints and Gramm-Rudman-Hollings automatic cuts, there is usefulness in *not* having information. With less information to identify the need for new housing, schools, and other publicly funded facilities, it is easier to ignore societal problems, easier to forget that the 1980s were a decade in which many Americans were counted out.

Buildings with fifty or more apartments often are public-housing projects, where two or three families may share an apartment. Special follow-up procedures are required to ensure that all inhabitants are counted. The effort will be nearly impossible, for not only will the bureau have insufficient funds but it faces the difficult task of temporarily hiring up to 500,000 enumerators at a time when the nation's unemployment rate is at a twenty-year low.

CRACKING THE I

Meet the new boss: Compute

America's is a postindustrial service economy, runs the conventional wisdom—an economy wherein the product is information and work occurs in a clean, well-lighted place. It's the age of the telemarketer, the customer-service rep, and the flight reservationist—all of whom rely on computer technology to do their jobs. Abuse of workers in this new economy would seem unlikely, but it's here, with age-old cruelty. Twenty-six million employees nationwide, from telephone operators to elevator mechanics, have their work tracked electronically. For ten million of these men and women, computer-generated statistical evaluations, such as the one shown here, are used to judge job performance and, it is held, to increase productivity. But the computer can't measure the physical and mental toll exacted by the stress of second-by-second surveillance. This printout evaluation records the day's work of one of the 350 airline reservationists huddled over computer terminals in the vast 100-by-100-foot reservations center at TWA's Chicago office. (To protect her $5.67-an-hour job, the agent's name has been removed.) To judge from the supervisor's handwritten comments, the agent has had a bad day.

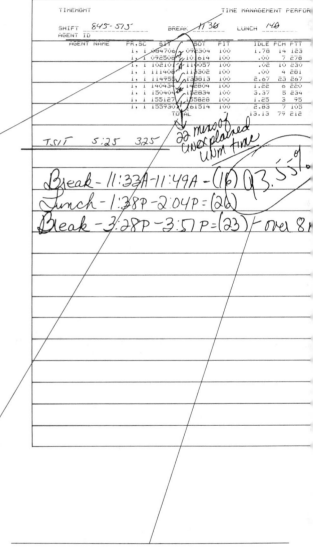

The supervisor has checked the gaps between SOT (sign-out time) and SIT (sign-in time). These gaps are known as UNM time, for unmanned time, a singularly inappropriate term: Most agents are women. "Unexplained" UNM time is almost always time spent in the bathroom. In this case, the reservationist's UNM time was unacceptably high because of an absence from 11:00 to 11:14—although we can all recall bathroom circumstances that required fourteen minutes or more, not to mention telephone calls to children sick at home. If the employee gets an urgent call from a babysitter or sick child, the message is relayed not to the employee but to the supervisor. To return urgent personal calls, employees must leave their work stations, thereby accruing UNM time, for even the most distraught mother dare not call home from her work phone, since the monitoring supervisor can listen to her call.

The supervisor has computed a "percent utilization" of 93.55 percent—an overall measure combining all the categories. It sounds like an exemplary level of productivity. But at this airline, rates below 96.5 percent trigger a series of disciplinary steps, such as a verbal or written warning ("a letter in your file") or even unpaid suspension if the number stays the same or falls lower in subsequent evaluations.

ECTRONIC WHIP
evaluation, *by Sharon Danann*

```
                    DATE  23 SEP 89      Sat
er                         SUPV  JUDYCKI
SWT  NOC    AOT  TNCH    TATT    TACW    What's this
  0    0   .00    14    2.05     .37     all
  0    1  2.07     7    4.64    2.36
  0    0   .00    10    3.83     .17
  0    0   .00     4    4.68     .05     too
  0    0   .00    23    4.45     .14
  0    0   .00     8    3.67     .08
  0    0   .00     5    3.71     .32     high
  0    0   .00     3    1.57     .33
  0    0   .00     7    1.74     .10
  0    1  2.07    79    3.53     .39     This helped
                                        pull this
Below Ave.                     341      times down!
S/O 228-302
M  415-515
```

- There is no excuse for this bad time management! You have complete control! Please make the necessary improvements Immediately !

The TACW, or total average after-call work—the paperwork for the tickets—has gotten this agent into extra trouble. Here she is being reprimanded for taking .39 minutes—about twenty-three seconds—to complete her paperwork for each call. The agent is damned if she does and damned if she doesn't; putting the customer on hold or engaging the customer in conversation in order to do paperwork will result in a higher TATT and can be observed by the eavesdropping supervisors.

TATT, or total average talk time, was three-and-a-half minutes over the course of the day. The length of each call is closely scrutinized. Think about this the next time you ask for three comparison fares or provide the detailed information required to send an unaccompanied small child to see grandparents. Reservationists cannot try to save time on customer calls by dropping an unnecessary sales pitch without risking additional discipline. Supervisors, who randomly listen to calls from a glass monitoring booth in the center of the reservations room, judge the calls strictly. If the supervisor challenges a particular call at the end of the day, the agent may be hard-pressed to remember it specifically. And she dare not commiserate with fellow workers—the supervisors can hear that, too.

TNCH is the total number of calls handled. Between her morning break and lunch, this agent took twenty-three calls for information or reservations, and a total of seventy-nine for the day. That sounds impressive, but it's considered low by management, which expects agents to handle 150 to 200 calls a day. The reservationist will be pressured daily to raise this number. Raw totals, and not customer needs, are what management is concerned with.

On television commercials, airline reservationists and their equivalents in other jobs are smiling, friendly, and boundlessly gratified by serving *you.* In reality, the agent has nothing approaching "complete control." The control lies with management and the ensuing threat is not an idle one. If the agent continues to have days like this, with problems in any of the monitored categories, she will be fired. And if that happens, she will be forced to look for another job in the electronic mills of the new economy.

Sharon Danann is the former research director of Cleveland-based 9to5, Working Women education fund, and author of the report "Stories of Mistrust and Manipulation: The Electronic Monitoring of the American Workforce."

A NATION OF CI

Federal gun registration neither protects n

Bureau of Alcohol, Tobacco, and Firearms Form 4473 is the only federal protection standing between you and anyone who wants to buy a gun and kill: nearly a quarter of the criminals who use guns buy them over-the-counter. Mandated by the 1968 Gun Control Act—something of a misnomer, since the law affords the government little control over gun production, sales, or ownership—the form must be filled out by buyers when they purchase a gun at one of the nation's 239,637 gun dealers. But although the bureau produces the forms, it is prohibited by law from using the completed forms to determine how many guns are sold and to whom. Nor does the bureau ensure that the forms are filled out correctly. It is the gun dealers who are responsible for making sure that applicants fill out the form—in reality, they make no attempt to verify buyers' answers—and it is the dealers who keep the forms on file. Thus, after Patrick Edward Purdy filled out this form last August 3, it simply remained with Clair Cooper, owner of the Sandy Trading Post.

> The "transferee" may buy the gun and then *legally* give it or sell it to anyone without further paperwork. When a new AK-47 was "transferred" to Patrick Purdy for $349.95, he kept it for himself.

When Congress passed the Gun Control Act, it didn't anticipate that Americans would desire to own civilian semi-automatic (each shot caused by a separate pull of the trigger) versions of military automatic (multiple firings caused by keeping the trigger depressed) weapons. Thus, the law allows the Russian-designed semi-automatic AK-47 to be categorized as a "rifle," even though the weapon is easily altered to be automatic. Typically, such weapons, which are often used by gangs and drug dealers, can fire 300 to 1,200 rounds a minute. Their bullets penetrate cars, walls, and police officers' vests. Law enforcement officials have long sought to outlaw assault rifles. The National Rifle Association insists the AK-47 and other assault rifles are used for "hunting" by hundreds of thousands of sportsmen. Even President Bush—a lifetime member of the NRA—seems to doubt this; in March his administration suspended imports of most semi-automatic weapons. Purdy, of course, had no intention of hunting.

Joseph D. McNamara is the former chief of police in San Jose, California, and the author of three novels, The First Directive, Fatal Command, *and* The Blue Mirage.

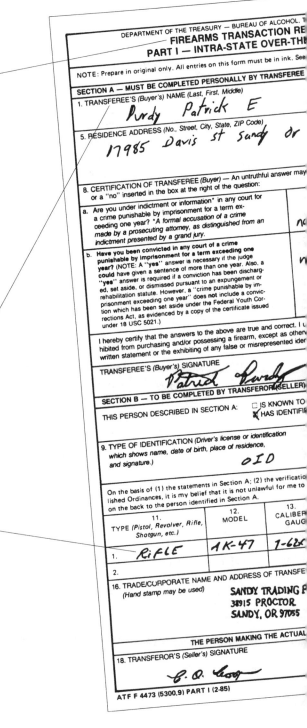

RTIFIED KILLERS

eters, by Police Chief Joseph D. McNamara

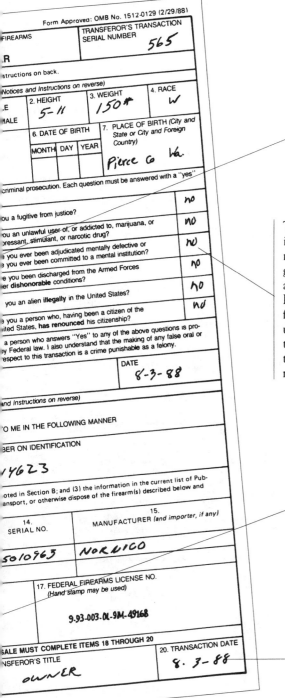

It's not hard to lie here, for if the answer is actually "yes," no one will know. Even a truthful "no" can have little meaning; although Purdy's response was technically correct, he had previously been charged with attempted robbery, criminal conspiracy, resisting arrest, illegal possession of a dangerous weapon, solicitation of sex, drug possession, receiving stolen property, and firing a pistol in a national forest. These charges were either plea-bargained down to misdemeanors or dropped.

The second part of this question requires a "yes" only if the buyer has been *involuntarily* committed to a mental institution; it does not probe further. A background check could have determined that Purdy had attempted suicide while in custody for a gun charge. He was also collecting Social Security disability benefits for drug abuse. That Patrick Purdy was mentally unstable became quite clear: a police search of his hotel room five months after he bought the AK-47 turned up toy soldiers, tanks, and jeeps all over the room, including in the refrigerator and shower.

Like most states, Oregon, where Purdy made his purchase, does not require a waiting period to enable the state to clear a buyer of a rifle or shotgun. Only Hawaii, Illinois, and Pennsylvania do. (A number of states require a waiting period for the purchase of handguns.) Yet state laws cannot guarantee sufficient protection: stronger federal legislation is required. California has one of the most stringent gun-control laws in the nation, but Purdy was able to purchase guns there.

On January 17, five months after signing this form in Sandy, Oregon, Purdy walked into the schoolyard of his former elementary school in Stockton, California, wearing a flak jacket, army fatigues, and earplugs. He then opened fire with his store-bought AK-47. In about six minutes he fired more than 100 rounds, killing five children and wounding twenty-nine children and a teacher. He then killed himself with a handgun that he had bought in California, after dutifully filling out another copy of this form.

Lunch at Le Cirque (in the Mayfair Regent Hotel, Sixty-fifth Street and Park Avenue), New York's most status-conscious restaurant: the menu is generally a mark of the parvenu, and is therefore most in evidence in the Siberian back reaches of the dining room, which seats 104. It rarely receives more than token glances from the regulars—among them, Richard Nixon, Roy Cohn, and Dustin Hoffman—wedged in at banquettes or huddled around center-aisle tables in the prestigious front bay (capacity: fifty), though Nancy Kissinger was seen recently studying one through a large magnifying glass. Regulars tend to know what they want. "I never look at the menu," says designer Mollie Parnes, whose teased blond hairdo *Women's Wear Daily* dubbed the Le Cirque Special.

Sirio Maccioni, the proprietor, was born in northern Italy, but knew when he opened Le Cirque in 1974 that French food (he is French-trained) was the only kind that would fetch top dollar—the daily lunchtime gross is $4,500—and attract the wealthy and the stylish. (He had developed a fashionable following at the Colony restaurant, where he was maitre d'.) The name "Le Cirque" was suggested by Ellen Lehman McCluskey, the society decorator who designed the dining room. To create the atmosphere she relied on murals of monkeys dressed as humans and aping social situations. No, Sirio says, he did not intend the monkeys as a commentary on his preening, chattering guests.

Lobster salad is the least profitable dish on the menu. It sells for $20.75 a la carte, but the ingredients are costly, and it takes a good deal of time to prepare. Nancy Reagan is likely to order the salad, but when she is at her hairdresser's (Monsieur Marc, 22 East Sixty-fifth Street) and doesn't have time to make it to the restaurant, Sirio sends over a chicken-and-watercress salad.

Déjeuner A La Carte

Hors D'Oeuvres

Bouquet de Fruits de Mer 9.75	Terrine de Canard aux Foie Gras et Pistaches 11.75
Saumon Fumé de Norvège 10.75	Gâteau de Légumes aux Coulis de Tomates 5.75
Truite et Esturgeon Fumé Petrossian 9.75	Terrine de Saumon aux Fruits de Mer 9.75
Salade de Crab Meat de Virginie aux Avocats 13.75	Terrine de Veau aux Herbes 7.75
Homards, Fonds d'Artichauts et Foie Gras 20.75	Tête et Pieds de Veau en Gelée 6.75
Choix de Coquillages 6.75	Jambon au Melon ou Figues en Saison 7.75
Salade de St. Jacques Fleurie 9.75	Foie Gras Truffé Maison 20.25
Red Snapper en Seviche 9.75	

Crème de Homard Fine Champagne 6.25	Velouté de Carotte Froid aux Ciboulettes 4.25
Potage du Jour 4.25	Consommé de Boeuf aux Paillettes 4.25

Oeufs Et Salades

Oeufs en Brioche à Votre Choix 12.75	Omelette Plate Bayonnaise 15.75
Omelette aux Foies de Volaille et Champignons 15.75	Oeufs Brouillés aux Truffes Blanches (en saison)
Omelette aux Fonds d'Artichauts et Fines Herbes 16.75	Omelette au Saumon Fumé et Fondue d'Oignons 16.75
Salade de Dindonneau Julienne 14.75	Salade de Dindonneau Julienne 14.75
Salade Santé au Miel 12.75	Sunset Salade 12.75
Salade de Homard Le Cirque 20.75	

Entrées

Sûpreme de Flounder Grillé Le Cirque 16.75
Goujonettes de Filet de Sole Frites Dijonnaise 15.75
Blanquettes de St. Jacques à l'Oseille 18.75
Quenelles de Brochet au Caviar de Saumon 18.75
Loup de l'Atlantique Grillé à l'Aneth 19.75
Sole de Douvre Grillé ou Sauté 21.75
Feuillantine de Saumon Venitienne 19.75
Filets de Soles Sautées aux Noisettes 17.75
Poulet ou Poussin Grillé Diable 16.25
Blancs de Volaille Champenoise 17.75
Poulet en Casserolle aux Oignons et Champignons 17.25
Magret de Canard aux Baies de Cassis et Gingembre 19.75
Escalopes de Veau Citron ou Milanaise 17.75
Rognon de Veau Sauté à l'Armagnac 18.75
Cervelle de Veau aux Câpres et Citron 15.75
Foie de Veau Sauté Fine Champagne et Raisin 17.75
Paillarde de Veau ou de Boeuf Grillé 20.75
Feuilles de Boeuf Toscane 15.75
Mignonette de Boeuf Sautées aux Champignons Sauvages 20.75
Entrecôte Poêlée à la Moelle 20.75
Deux Mignons d'Agneau Grillé aux Herbes 20.75

VIN CARAFE

Blanc - Rouge

La Carafe 14.50   La Demi 7.50

Cover $1.50

Mimi Sheraton is the food editor of Condé Nast Traveler *and the former food critic for* Time. *She publishes the newsletter* Mimi Sheraton's Taste *and is currently writing guides to New York restaurants and United States restaurants.*

"Déjeuner" is the operative word. Lunch is a far more crackling scene than dinner, though the night meal brings with it a share of waving, kiss-blowing, and table hopping. Regulars lunch at 12:30 P.M., and usually order a la carte, not table d'hôte. But when they run up a la carte bills with selections that have less expensive table d'hôte equivalents, Sirio charges the cheaper fixed price: $26.25 (drinks excluded, of course). "Especially the women," he says. "Women like a bargain."

Le Cirque's most famous entree, pasta primavera, never appears on the menu. Kitchen snobbery keeps the dish hidden. "My French chefs think it would make us look like a spaghetti joint," Sirio says. Pasta primavera is priced at $15.75 ($9.75 as an appetizer), and is ordered by about fifty people each day. Mary Lasker could be seen recently consuming a large portion without ever removing her mink coat.

English makes a rare appearance with this dish, in which "sunset" refers to California—the *salade* combines oranges, avocados, and nuts. Other English intrusions include "golden oysters," "orange surprise," and "cover," which at lunch is $1.50.

Herbed roast chicken in a casserole (a la carte price: $17.25) is the most profitable dish on the menu. The ingredients cost little, and the casserole is relatively simple to prepare. Those blessed with hearty appetites, among them Henry Kissinger, prefer this dish to, say, Sunset Salade.

Petits fours are priced at $4, but no one is charged for them. Regulars call them free cookies, and one, Nancy Reagan buddy and escort-about-town Jerry Zipkin, has been known to stuff his pockets with them.

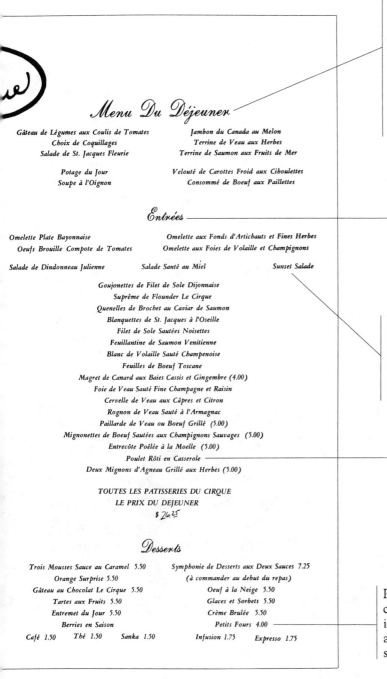

Menu Du Déjeuner

Gâteau de Légumes aux Coulis de Tomates	Jambon du Canada au Melon
Choix de Coquillages	Terrine de Veau aux Herbes
Salade de St. Jacques Fleurie	Terrine de Saumon aux Fruits de Mer
Potage du Jour	Velouté de Carottes Froid aux Ciboulettes
Soupe à l'Oignon	Consommé de Boeuf aux Paillettes

Entrées

Omelette Plate Bayonnaise   Omelette aux Fonds d'Artichauts et Fines Herbes
Oeufs Brouille Compote de Tomates   Omelette aux Foies de Volaille et Champignons

Salade de Dindonneau Julienne   Salade Santé au Miel   Sunset Salade

Goujonettes de Filet de Sole Dijonnaise
Suprême de Flounder Le Cirque
Quenelles de Brochet au Caviar de Saumon
Blanquettes de St. Jacques à l'Oseille
Filet de Sole Sautées Noisettes
Feuillantine de Saumon Venitienne
Blanc de Volaille Sauté Champenoise
Feuilles de Boeuf Toscane
Magret de Canard aux Baies Cassis et Gingembre (4.00)
Foie de Veau Sauté Fine Champagne et Raisin
Cervelle de Veau aux Câpres et Citron
Rognon de Veau Sauté à l'Armagnac
Paillarde de Veau ou Boeuf Grillé (5.00)
Mignonettes de Boeuf Sautées aux Champignons Sauvages (5.00)
Entrecôte Poêlée à la Moelle (5.00)
Poulet Rôti en Casserole
Deux Mignons d'Agneau Grillé aux Herbes (5.00)

TOUTES LES PATISSERIES DU CIRQUE
LE PRIX DU DEJEUNER
$ 26.25

Desserts

Trois Mousses Sauce au Caramel 5.50	Symphonie de Desserts aux Deux Sauces 7.25
Orange Surprise 5.50	(à commander au debut du repas)
Gâteau au Chocolat Le Cirque 5.50	Oeuf à la Neige 5.50
Tartes aux Fruits 5.50	Glaces et Sorbets 5.50
Entremet du Jour 5.50	Crème Brulée 5.50
Berries en Saison	Petits Fours 4.00

Café 1.50   Thé 1.50   Sanka 1.50   Infusion 1.75   Expresso 1.75

This is it. Playing the Palace. Numero uno, not only status-wise but historically—it was the *New York Times* that published the first weekly best-seller list, on Sunday, October 9, 1942. There are other lists: the one compiled by the *Los Angeles Times* is not sniffed at; an appearance there may ignite the attention of a dozing film magnate. And the list in *Publishers Weekly* gets read by the trade. But the *Times* . . . a mention even near the bottom of the list is regarded as a force equal to that of a full-page ad in the *Book Review*. It also provides a priceless opportunity to witness that most cherished (and lucrative) of publishing phenomena, the Self-Fulfilling Prophecy. An appearance on the list is likely to inspire one's publisher to recommend an infusion of money into one's book's ad budget, and to encourage booksellers to erect displays—actions taken, in other words, so best sellers might best sell.

It is a fact that people buy best-selling fiction because it happens to be best-selling. Once an author has nailed his flag to the top of the greasy pole, it is likely to spank smartly in the breeze for quite a little while. We are talking hard-bound novels here—paperbacks have their own list, and appearances by collections of short stories, while not unheard of (Welty, Bradbury, Cheever), are rare. It doesn't take much for a novel to make the list—maybe 30,000 copies during a slow summer. The top of the heap is another matter. By mid-January of this year, there were 885,000 copies of *The Talisman* in print, perhaps for use as doorstops.

Herewith, a noble attempt to identify a few books that are actually worth reading. Nobody knows if having one's book singled out as an "editors' choice" does any good beyond confirming what one already knew. But bear this in mind: it is not unheard of to discover no fewer than two books by *Times* staffers here. This week, of particular interest, find books by Alan Riding (the paper's bureau chief in Brazil) and Leonard Silk (its economics columnist).

L. J. Davis is a contributing editor of Harper's Magazine.

OF LISTS

ead and golden? by L. J. Davis

There were 1.1 million copies of Lee Iacocca's autobiography in print when this list appeared, which would seem to prove that if one wants to write a best seller, one should leave the writing to someone else. *Iacocca* isn't even a real ghosted autobiography; it is a series of occasionally entertaining, selectively sanitized anecdotes and after-dinner speeches in which, with astonishing vigor, the chairman of Chrysler does not run for president of the United States.

Once a best seller has been written—or, in the cases of Iacocca and John Madden, not written—how is it found, counted, *made*? This was long a source of mystery. Actually, compiling the list is simplicity itself: each week, some 2,000 bookstores, carefully selected in an effort to achieve balance in terms of location and size, receive three lists of hard-cover contenders: two of thirty-six each (fiction and nonfiction), one of twelve ("Advice, How-to and Miscellaneous"). Each bookseller is asked to arrange the week's picks in order of sales, adding any unlisted shooting stars that have appeared in his sales figures. At an appointed moment, the *Times* calls and asks for the tally. . .

. . . and then, it "statistically adjusts" its findings—a process that has reduced William Peter Blatty, for one, to a state bordering on incoherence. In August 1983, Blatty sued the *Times* when his novel *Legion* failed to make the list in sufficiently gratifying fashion—this despite its breathless prose and (more important) mega-big (he believed) sales. The *Book Review*'s adjustment, called weighting, works this way: if there are ten bookstores in a region, and the *Times* is in touch with three of them, each book sold by these stores is assigned a value of three and one third. Presumably, this gives a fairly reliable picture of national sales while winnowing out purely local phenomena. All this numbers-crunching is necessary because publishers gleefully release some sales figures while guarding others as though they were the Koh-i-noor. Which leads, quickly and neatly, to this question: If the publishers don't want to play, and there are authors who think the game is rigged, why not drop the whole thing?

ALL THE PRE

The perquisites of the pre

At 8 P.M. on Wednesday, June 11, the stage was set for President Reagan's thirty-seventh press conference. Because his unscripted encounters with the press are often adventures in garbled facts and rambling answers, the White House attempts to orchestrate as much as possible—the President's answers as well as the choice of reporters who will ask the questions. Reagan spent the better part of two days preparing for this occasion. He answered questions from aides posing as reporters and he studied this seating chart, prepared by the White House. White House spokesman Larry Speakes insists that "there really is no grand design," but certain reporters and news organizations are assigned the best seats, and thus have the best chance to ask questions. Of the more than 100 reporters in attendance on June 11, Reagan called on thirteen.

Helen Thomas of UPI is one of the few reporters assured of the President's nod. By a tradition among reporters that dates back to Franklin Roosevelt's administration, the two major wire services—AP and UPI—get the first two questions. On June 11, Thomas began the conference by asking Reagan about the status of SALT II, which she considered "the most pressing issue of the day."

NBC's Andrea Mitchell used to be among the favored few. Along with ABC's Sam Donaldson and CBS's Lesley Stahl or Bill Plante, she was routinely assigned a front-row seat. For a network correspondent, this virtually guarantees the chance to ask a question. (Speakes calls this practice "modern traditional," since it began during the tenure of Richard Nixon.) But Mitchell recently lost out when her celebrated colleague Chris Wallace negotiated a new contract with NBC that grants him exclusive first-row rights. Mitchell is now consigned to the back rows, which, to White House officials and reporters, are known as "Siberia."

Eleanor Clift is a congressional and political correspondent for Newsweek.

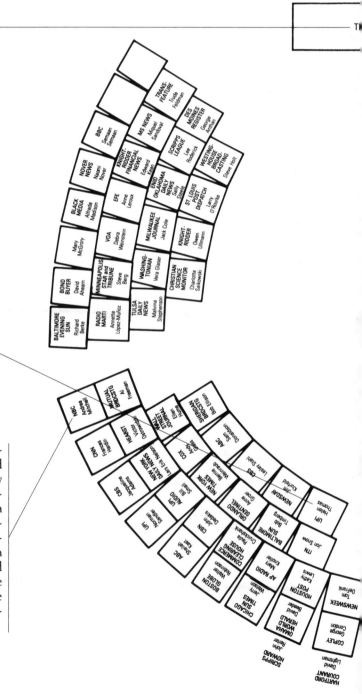

DENT'S NODS

onference, *by Eleanor Clift*

Early on, the White House press corps discovered that the President is partial to red, Nancy's favorite color. On press conference nights even the grayest male reporters sparkle with red. One who opted for this strategy on June 11 was Lester Kinsolving, a specialist in embarrassing questions, whom Reagan tries to avoid. In the third row, Kinsolving sported a red blazer, but Reagan passed over him for the reporter "with the red flower," the *Buffalo News*'s Max McCarthy. The White House, thinking Mc-Carthy a safer choice, had put him in the first row.

The three major newsmagazines—*Time*, *Newsweek*, and *U.S. News*—play a game of musical chairs in the first, second, and third rows. On June 11 it was *Time*'s turn to sit in the front row, but David Beckwith wanted to make sure he was also on Reagan's handwritten list—the one on the three-by-five card the President carries with him to the podium. Beckwith told Speakes he wanted to ask Reagan about Star Wars, *Time*'s cover story that week. Speakes agreed, seeing Star Wars as an ideal press conference "softball." The President, however, never got around to Beckwith.

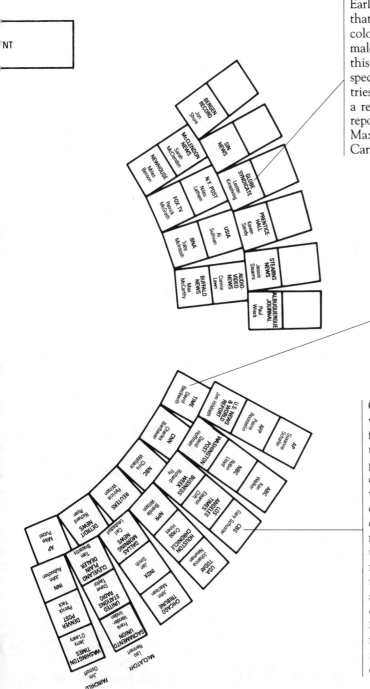

Gary Schuster, despite his distant vantage point, was the fourth questioner recognized. As a reporter for the *Detroit News*, he covered the 1980 presidential campaign; his irreverent wit and Marlboro Man good looks made him a favorite with both the President and Nancy. Schuster's professional stock rose when Reagan repeatedly sought him out at press conferences, and CBS hired him last year. (He didn't, however, survive the layoffs in July.) Tonight, Schuster asked Reagan what he thought of that day's Supreme Court decision upholding the right to abortion. Reagan misunderstood the question even though he asked Schuster to repeat it, and gave his response to another Court decision concerning the rights of handicapped infants. The Supreme Court miscue typified Reagan's poor performance overall. Later, commenting on his showing, he said that in concentrating on whom to call on he had forgotten what he was supposed to say.

FAINT LIGHT

Roy Cohn, AIDS, and the que

Roy Cohn died August 2 at the Warren Grant Magnuson Clinical Center of the National Institutes of Health, in Bethesda, Maryland. The primary cause of death was listed as "cardio-pulmonary arrest"; the death certificate named "dementia" and "underlying HTLV-3 infections" as secondary causes. The mention of HTLV-3 implied what many suspected: Roy Cohn had AIDS. Cohn's NIH records—leaked to me last summer and published here, in part, for the first time— confirm he knew as early as last November that he had AIDS. But like other public figures who have contracted the disease, Cohn never admitted to having it. Not all of the problems and complications associated with AIDS are medical; journalists are having a difficult time writing about it, drawing a plausible distinction between private and public information. Their dilemma raises questions about what society wants, or doesn't want, to know about itself.

Cohn was admitted last November 4 to an AIDS treatment program at the NIH center. It is a publicly funded program, and one not easy to gain admission to. Sources at NIH told me that Cohn used his political influence in Washington—he counted the Reagans among his friends—to get into the program. Reporting on political favors is a staple of American newspapers, but when such reporting has to do with AIDS, there arises a problem of judgment. What matters most: publishing (making public) or privacy? And should privacy be respected if the individual whose privacy is at issue is getting favored treatment with public money?

"Companion Peter Fraisure" is Peter Frazier. He has been described in the press during the past year as the office manager in Cohn's law firm, and as one of Cohn's travel companions. Lois Romano, writing in the *Washington Post* last December, described Frazier as "the one who brings the evening to an end when he sees Cohn drooping." Frazier often accompanied Cohn when he went to the center for his treatments.

PATIENT

PATIENT NAME: COHN
NURSING UNIT: OP12
BED NUMBER:
INST/BR: C MI
REGISTRY NO: 18-
ADMITTED: 11/
ATTENDING MD: YOU
ADMIT DX: SAF

HOME ADDRESS: 39
NEW
10

NEXT OF KIN:
DATE OF BIRTH: 02

COHN, ROY MARCUS
11/
12:00NN 102 (CCAK)
12:00NN 36.5 (CCAK
11/

01:00PM SEXUALITY
INFORMATION ON SEX
STATED THAT THE SA
THAT IF HE WANTED
NEED TO USE A CON
INFORM HIS PARTNE
DID STRESS THAT H
SEX WITH THIS DIS
PROTOCOL. (CCAK)

COHN, ROY MARCUS
1

11:00PM SOCIO/PS
REMEMBERS GOING
THE DETAILS. INS
MEDICATIONS REVI
PETER FRAISURE.
11:00PM MOBILITY
TOLERATED WELL.
11:00PM NEURO/S
ALWAYS ORIENTED
HOME IN AM. GAI
TREMORS CONTINU
(DTAF)

ROY MARCU

DARK PRINT

n of privacy, *by Dale Van Atta*

PRINT

MARCUS

-6
12:42PM
ROBERT C
..

8TH ST.
K, NY

27

P-R
T-O

--PT ASKED FOR
RACTICES. I
SEX WAS NONE BUT
AVE SEX HE WOULD
ND ESPECIALLY
T HE HAD AIDS. I
ULD ABSTAIN FROM
AND ON THIS

85
OGICAL OBSV --
TOMORROW. MIXES UP
IONS AND
WITH COMPANION
=)
V --OUT ON PASS
F)
Y OBSV --ALERT. NOT
Y AWARE WILL GO
GHT SHUFFLE. HAND
PROBLEMS THIS PM.

3/85
BY FRIEND WITH RX

During an interview with Mike Wallace aired last March on *60 Minutes*, Cohn categorically denied that he had AIDS. "We were told [that your] name was on the NIH computer for AIDS," Wallace said. "Well, I shouldn't be," Cohn said. "I'll get that taken care of very fast." Cohn said he had cancer, and in a sense he did. He had Kaposi's sarcoma, the cancer to which AIDS victims, with profoundly impaired immune systems, are extremely vulnerable. Wallace did not press the matter, as he often does. Newsmen find it hard enough simply to raise the question.

Rumors that Roy Cohn was a homosexual first appeared in the 1950s, when he was the communist-hunting chief counsel to Senator Joseph McCarthy. Cohn, another young McCarthy investigator, G. David Schine, and McCarthy were all bachelors, and very devoted to one another—Lillian Hellman called them "Bonnie, Bonnie, and Clyde." Cohn always denied to reporters that he was "ever gay-inclined," and went out of his way to convey an impression of heterosexual orthodoxy. He would talk of having discussed marriage with Barbara Walters. And he was a lawyer for the Roman Catholic Archdiocese of New York, which vociferously opposed New York City's gay-civil-rights legislation.

In the descriptions of Cohn in her *Post* story, Romano noted that his right hand and shoulder would often shake, that he moved "as if in slow-motion." These symptoms can be associated with AIDS, but not with liver cancer, the disease from which Cohn claimed to be suffering. Romano was apparently doing the best she could—legally and, by today's standards, ethically—to tell her readers that Cohn was lying.

Dale Van Atta, with Jack Anderson, writes the nationally syndicated column "Washington Merry-Go-Round."

33

According to NIH medical personnel I have spoken with—and as noted in the medical report here—Cohn was "somewhat reluctant to become celibate." AIDS is a lethal disease, and certain sexual acts—in particular, anal intercourse—apparently facilitate transmission of the virus. Did members of the public, especially someone who might have become a sex partner of Cohn's, have a right to know that he had AIDS? If Cohn was reluctant to become celibate *and* reluctant to tell the truth, did journalists have a right (an *obligation*) to publish the truth?

Cohn was not above using his illness, however misleading his testimony, when it could help him muster sympathy. His lawyers in his disbarment case—he was disbarred from the practice of law in New York State six weeks before his death—pleaded for leniency on the grounds that he was too ill to continue in his profession. No medical certificate was ever presented describing his ailment. The press never made an issue of it.

Azidothymidine (AZT) is one of the brightest hopes for AIDS patients; the drug has been shown in some cases to hold the virus at bay. Only a limited number of AIDS patients in government-approved testing programs received the drug. Of the more than 10,000 people thought to be dying of AIDS last spring, only twenty-eight had access to AZT through NIH programs. Cohn was one of the fortunate. Did he use his Washington connections to obtain the drug? A private matter, or a public one?

11:00PM NEURO/
ALWAYS ORIENTED. VERY
HOME IN AM. GAIT SLIGH
TREMORS CONTINUE. NO P
(DTAF)

ROY MARCUS
11/23/

11:00AM ACCOMPANIED B
MEDS (CCAK)
11:00AM PT DISCHARGED
11:00AM GOALS-PT WILL
OF BODY FLUIDS WITH
PLAN-REINFORC
CELIBATE STATE CAUTIO
DISEASE. (CCAK)

11:00AM SEXUALITY.
ASSESSMENT-
HAVE SEX WITH ANY O
POSSIBLE TRANSMISSI
PROBLEMS/NU
STATD SOMEWHAT RELU
CELIBATE. (CCAK)
11:00AM SOCIO/PSYCH
(CCAK)
11:00AM SAFETY STAT
11:00AM PROBLEMS/N
SUPERVISION AT HOM
ABILITY TO AMBULAT
ADMISSION. (CCAK)

11:00AM MOBILITY S
PENDENT: STAIRS, N
TRANSFER, INDEPEND
TOLERANCE-DOES TIF
11:00AM PROBLEMS/N
AT HOME TO PREPARE
IDENTIFIED. (CCAK

11:00AM FOOD/FLUI
PENDENT: FOOD PRE
HIGH PROTEIN: APP

11:00AM CIRCULATI
100: BP-170/100:
PROBLEMS
GOALS-AT
DEFERRED DUE TO
LOFE STYLE CHANG
INAPPORPRIATE FO
(CCAK)
11:00AM AIR STAT
11:00AM CURRENT
(CCAK)

11:00AM DISCHAR
CRITERI
CIRCUMSTANCES P
HEALTH PROFESSI
QUESTIONS REGAR
REQUIREMENTS OF
STATUS: STATES
PROFESSIONAL F
INCREASED COUG
WEST 12TH FLO
CALLENDER. NUM
HOME DIRECTION
ACTION, ADMINIS

WILL GO
FFLE. HAND
MS THIS PM.

END WITH RX

ING (CCAK)
HAVE EXCHANGE
THER PERSON..
EDS FOR
AINST PREAD OF

UTIONED NOT TO
NO SINCE
THE DISEASE..
DIAGNOSIS-PT
TO BECOME

ICAL STATUS

CCAK)
AGNOSIS-HAS
H SERVANTS BUT
INCREASED SINCE

; WALKING, INDE
ASSIST;
ACTIVITY
SILY (CCAK)
IAGNOSIS-HAS COOK
LS SO NO NEEDS

TUS; FEEDING, INDE
NABLE TO DO; DIET-
-FAIR (CCAK)
TATUS; PULSE(S) -
R-PINK.
DX-HYPERTENSION.
TIME THIS WAS
RRENT PROGNOSIS
ULD BE
IS--PROGNOSIS.

RATE-20 (CCAK)
TH STATUS SUMMARY

LANNING SUMMARY.
TATES UNDER WHICH
EDS TO CONTACT A
& WHERE TO CALL FOR
PROTOCOL
NGE IN HEALTH
TO CONTACT HEALTH
VER INFECTON
ERSON TO CONTACT-12
LINIC OR DR.
WRITTEN DOWN AS TAKE
STATE(S) MEDICATION,
DOSAGE,SCHED, (CCAK)

Cohn had many friends in the press who chose to defend or simply leave unchallenged his lies and evasions. William Safire, in the *New York Times*, denounced the July 25 column Jack Anderson and I wrote about Cohn's AZT treatment: "Doctors with some sense of medical ethics and journalists with some regard for a core of human privacy are shamed by [this] investigative excess." The *New York Post* usually carries the column, but didn't publish that one.

Only after Cohn's death, in his obituaries, was it widely reported that he had AIDS. Even that was something of a show of nerve—readers of the *New York Times* and other big-city papers learn of young men dying of "pneumonia" or after a "long illness," but not of an AIDS-related illness. The *Times's* in-house publication, *Winners and Sinners*, noted recently with regard to the paper's obituaries that "some suspect us of shrinking from our duty to report on an epidemic." There are a few bold patients dying of AIDS who have sought to expose their illness to public discussion. Obituaries of makeup artist Way Bandy noted that he had requested mention be made that he died of AIDS. Most remarkable was an editorial published in the *Honolulu Star-Bulletin* on September 1. The paper's managing editor, Bill Cox, announced he was going on disability leave because he had AIDS. He wrote that "as a journalist I have spent my career trying to shed light in dark corners. AIDS is surely one of our darkest corners. It can use some light."

Château Cos d'Estournel is owned by M. Bruno Prats. The wine he makes, like almost all clarets from Bordeaux, is valued for its elegance and ability to improve with age. This ability commands a price: as a Bordeaux moves from barrel to bottle to cellar, costs accrue. Sometimes, the final price is very high—a bottle of Château Lafite-Rothschild, 1961, from the cellar of Sherry-Lehmann, on Madison Avenue, costs $395. A bottle of newly arrived Château Cos d'Estournel, 1983 vintage, can be purchased in a liquor store for about $25. Prats doesn't set this price. He establishes only the opening price, by offering for sale his *première tranche*, or "first slice," of new wine, in the spring following harvest. In the spring of 1986, Prats announced the price of his '85 vintage: eighty-five francs (roughly $13) a bottle.

The price of a Bordeaux is still determined to an extent by the classifications established by the merchants of the Bordeaux wine exchange 131 years ago. The phrase *grand cru classé en 1855* means the grapes on this estate were considered to be a great growth, or crop. There was a further ranking done: first, second, third, fourth, fifth growth. First growths are the Cadillacs—Château Haut-Brion, Lafite, Latour, Margaux, Mouton Rothschild— and are identified on their labels as *premier cru*. Cos d'Estournel is a second growth. Like all vintners whose estates do not have first-growth ranking, Prats chooses simply to drape his wine in the generous and profitable *grand cru* cloak.

Prats's estate is widely regarded as producing the best wine in the commune of St.-Estèphe. In an average year, the estate produces 300,000 bottles—a lot of wine, but only a trickle in the torrent (679,000,000 bottles!) now imported into the United States each year from around the world. Still, limited production and unflagging demand mean there's a seller's market for classified Bordeaux. The vintner normally sells his new wine to a *courtier*, a sort of broker, who then finds a *negociant* (no problem with a good Bordeaux) and sells the wine to him—earning a commission of 2 or 3 percent. In turn, the *negociant* (a wholesaler and exporter) easily lines up an importer, a deal for which he takes his 10 percent.

S OF BORDEAUX

ctus, by Tom Maresca

Estate-bottling is costly—this, as much as anything else, is why you pay more for a Bordeaux than for jug wine. There is all the equipment (holding tanks, fermenters, oak barrels, temperature-control systems), and all the time: it takes three years to age a claret to the point where it can be marketed. The Kobrand Corporation, a New York-based importer of Cos d'Estournel, in effect loses two or three years' interest on its money—the price it paid to the *negociant*–before it actually has the wine to sell. Kobrand also absorbs the costs of transatlantic freight, insurance, taxes, and trucking. To turn a profit, the importer will add anywhere from 20 to 30 percent to the price of the wine it sells to regional wholesalers and distributors.

Bordeaux's *grands crus* sit atop what you might think of as an AOC (*Appellation d'Origine Contrôlée*) pyramid, the base of which is unclassified Bordeaux, red or white, and the middle layers wines designated by more precise and narrow geographical labeling. The AOC notation primarily guarantees that a wine actually comes from the region and/or estate proclaimed on its label—there has never been a phony Cos d'Estournel, as far as I know. But a few years ago, a counterfeit Mouton turned up in the United States, and in the early 1970s there was a much greater scandal involving reputable shippers bottling wine from the Midi and selling it as unclassified Bordeaux.

The wholesalers and distributors who buy their Cos d'Estournel from Kobrand will mark up the price about 30 percent before selling it to retailers. Your liquor store, in turn, will tack on from 30 percent (standard) to 50 percent, which would seem excessive if it weren't for the example set by restaurateurs. Restaurant markups often test the limits of rapacity: 100 percent above the wholesale price is normal, 200 percent not unusual, more than that by no means unknown. In 1988, when Prats's '85 vintage will be available, expect to pay anywhere from $26 to $33 at the liquor store. To drink it right away, however, would be a mistake. It needs a few years to lose its harshness and deepen and soften to classic Bordeaux elegance.

Tom Maresca is the author of The Right Wine, *recently published by Grove-Weidenfeld.*

GREAT SHOW, N

Running for the Senate is a co

Alan Cranston, Democrat of California, has been a U.S. senator since 1968, and no doubt believes his presence on the Senate floor is worth a great deal—roughly $12 million, which is what he is expected to spend in his attempt to be reelected this fall. Getting elected to the Senate has always been work; now it is a business, and a crucial part of the business is raising campaign funds. Having plenty of money on hand may not guarantee victory—but not having enough nearly always spells defeat.

Most candidates still raise the majority of their campaign funds from individual donors, and Cranston is no exception. In fact, he has made a serious attempt to attract small donors; his re-election committee says that some 80 percent of his contributors give $100 or less. The rationale for encouraging this kind of giving is that the more people who contribute to a campaign, the deeper the grass-roots support for the candidate (and the stronger the populist image). Direct-mail solicitation letters and telephone banks are generally used to raise money from individual donors. Cranston, who has a reputation as an effective and hardworking fund-raiser, helps draft the solicitation letters and has been known to work the telephones. He also attends breakfast, lunch, and dinner fund-raisers. Last June, for example, he raised $225,000 in a single evening from more than 100 supporters who met at the Washington, D.C., home of Averell Harriman.

Contributions to Senate candidates from political action committees amounted to $30 million in 1983–84, and could top $40 million in this election. By the end of 1985, Cranston had raised more than $500,000 from PACs. Labor union PACs figure big in this total; among the earliest contributors to his 1986 campaign were PACs run by the American Federation of Teachers, the Communications Workers of America, and the International Brotherhood of Painters & Allied Trades. Cranston's voting record, as far as unions are concerned? The AFL-CIO gives him a 92 percent lifetime rating. But business helps to bankroll Cranston too, despite a Chamber of Commerce rating of only 16 percent. Incumbents, natural favorites in most races, receive approximately 60 percent of PAC monies in Senate contests.

Jeremy Gaunt is a journalist with Reuters in New York.

DETAILED SU
of Receipts and
(Page 2, FE

Name of Committee (in Full)
Cranston for Senate '86

I. RECEIPTS

11. CONTRIBUTIONS (other than loans) FROM:
(a) Individuals/Persons Other Than Political Committees
(Memo Entry Unitemized $ **1,383,720**
(b) Political Party Committees
(c) Other Political Committees
(d) The Candidate
(e) TOTAL CONTRIBUTIONS (other than loans (add 11 (a), 11 (b), 11 (c)
and 11 (d))

12. TRANSFERS FROM OTHER AUTHORIZED COMMITTEES

13. LOANS:
(a) Made or Guaranteed by the Candidate
(b) All Other Loans
(c) TOTAL LOANS (add 13 (a) and 13 (b))

14. OFFSETS TO OPERATING EXPENDITURES (Refunds, Rebates, etc.)

15. OTHER RECEIPTS (Dividends, Interest, etc.)

16. TOTAL RECEIPTS (add 11 (e), 12, 13 (c), 14 and 15)

II. DISBURSEMENTS

17. OPERATING EXPENDITURES

18. TRANSFERS TO OTHER AUTHORIZED COMMITTEES

19. LOAN REPAYMENTS:
(a) Of Loans Made or Guaranteed by the Candidate
(b) Of All Other Loans
(c) TOTAL LOAN REPAYMENTS (add 19 (a) and 19 (b))

20. REFUNDS OF CONTRIBUTIONS TO:
(a) Individuals/Persons Other Than Political Committees
(b) Political Party Committees
(c) Other Political Committees
(d) TOTAL CONTRIBUTION REFUNDS (add 20 (a), 20 (b) an

21. OTHER DISBURSEMENTS

22. TOTAL DISBURSEMENTS (add 17, 18, 19 (c), 20 (d) and 21)

III. CASH SUMMARY

23. CASH ON HAND AT BEGINNING OF REPORTING PERIOD

24. TOTAL RECEIPTS THIS PERIOD (From Line 16)

25. SUBTOTAL (Add Line 23 and Line 24)

26. TOTAL DISBURSEMENTS THIS PERIOD (From Line 22)

27. CASH ON HAND AT CLOSE OF THE REPORTING PERIO

CHEAP SEATS

proposition, *by Jeremy Gaunt*

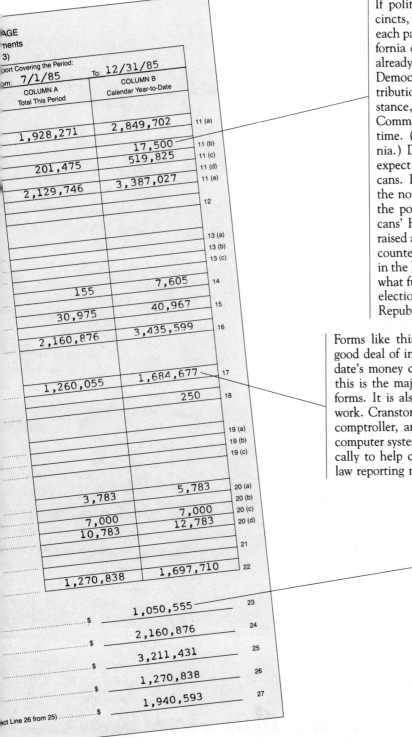

If political parties can no longer deliver precincts, they can still reach into their pockets—each party can spend up to $1.7 million in California on a senatorial candidate. Cranston has already gotten a good deal more in kind from the Democrats than the $17,500 in direct cash contributions listed here; earlier this year, for instance, the Democratic Senatorial Campaign Committee bought him $300,000 worth of TV time. (TV is crucial in big states like California.) Democratic candidates, however, cannot expect their party to ante up like the Republicans. Fund-raising has given new meaning to the notion that the Democrats are the party of the poor: in the 1984 elections, the Republicans' House and Senate campaign committees raised a total of $140 million. Their Democratic counterparts? $19 million. It's a dangerous gap: in the last weeks of a heated campaign, money is what fuels a big push. Of the last fifteen Senate elections decided by 4 percentage points or less, Republicans have won all but two.

Forms like this filed with the FEC provide a good deal of information about where a candidate's money comes from and where it goes—this is the major benefit of post-Watergate reforms. It is also a major new source of paperwork. Cranston's campaign has a full-time paid comptroller, an accountant on retainer, and a computer system with software designed specifically to help candidates meet federal-election-law reporting requirements.

An incumbent with plenty of cash on hand—someone like Senator Alfonse D'Amato, Republican of New York, who at the end of last year had more than $4 million at his disposal—can all but scare off a serious challenger. Cranston has had no such luck. He is facing one of the toughest battles of his political life: his opponent, California Congressman Ed Zschau, is young (forty-six), attractive, and well-backed. It will be one of the most expensive election fights in history. There are no spending limits in Senate races, as there are in publicly funded presidential races. The Supreme Court ruled ten years ago that campaign spending is essentially a form of free speech. In California this fall, as elsewhere around the nation, the Bill of Rights is being fully exercised.

DILEMMA IN SW

Surrogate mothers, natural fath

This is page one of a six-page contract that this winter became one of the most controversial of any in the country—the contract that led to the birth of Baby M and the battle for her custody. Over the past ten years, a few surrogate mothers have refused to give up their babies (so far, more than 500 babies have been born to surrogate mothers); but no father until William Stern has fought for custody—and in so doing, remanded to the courts a matter of profound legal, emotional, and moral complexity. No matter who ultimately wins custody of Baby M—the case could be in the courts for some time—a morass of issues remains untouched.

Couples turn to a surrogate mother when the woman is infertile or pregnancy poses a threat to her health— Elizabeth Stern has a mild case of multiple sclerosis— and yet the couple wants a child who is biologically related to at least one parent, the father. But "fatherhood" is legally ambiguous; until recently, paternity could not even be proven medically. And court records reflect a history of paternal denial: fathers happy to grant custody of their children to the wives they are divorcing; fathers leaving a state to avoid child-support payments. Moreover, of the twenty-nine states with laws governing artificial insemination—a process in which the natural father, in effect, is the surrogate—twelve bar the sperm-donor from any paternal claim. Should the rules be different when the donor-father arranges to make a baby?

We regard a woman's relationship with her baby as commencing with conception. And until very recently the courts have presumed that mothers are best suited to raise small children. But is this "nature's" way? What of mothers who put their children up for adoption? Where do infanticide and abortion fit into this? And what about the hundreds of surrogate mothers who have had little problem with the arrangement? Further complicating the situation are the possible ramifications should the courts decide that women have a "special" right to babies they give birth to. Would it perpetuate women's traditional responsibility to bring up babies and forgo careers?

Judith Levine is the author of My Enemy, My Love: Exploring Man-Hating in Women's Lives (Doubleday) *and is a columnist for* New York Woman *magazine.*

SURROGATE PARENTING AG

THIS AGREEMENT is made this **6th** day of

MARY BETH WHITEHEAD, a married woman (herein refer

her husband (herein referred to as a "Husband"),

"Natural Father").

RECITALS

THIS AGREEMENT is made with references

(1) WILLIAM STERN, Natural Father, is

years who is desirous of entering into this Agree

(2) The sole purpose of this Agreement

infertile wife to have a child which is biologic

(3) MARY BETH WHITEHEAD, Surrogate, a

the age of eighteen (18) years and desirous of e

of the following:

NOW THEREFORE, in consideration of th

intentions of being legally bound hereby, the p

1. MARY BETH WHITEHEAD, Surrogate, r

children. MARY BETH WHITEHEAD understands and

she will not form or attempt to form a parent-

she may conceive, carry to term and give birth

Agreement, and shall freely surrender custody

upon birth of the child; and terminate all par

Agreement.

2. MARY BETH WHITEHEAD, Surrogate,

married since 12/2/73, and RICHARD WHITEHEAD

provisions of this Agreement and acknowledges

shall be artificially inseminated pursuant to

WHITEHEAD agrees that in the best inrrerest of

a parent-child relationship with any child o

conceive by artificial insemination as descr

surrender immediate custody of the child to

parental rights; RICHARD WHITEHEAD further a

rebut the presumption of paternity of any o

aforementioned agreement as provided by law

3. WILLIAM STERN, Natural Fathe

Agreement with MARY BETH WHITEHEAD, Surrog

artificially inseminated with the semen of

WHITEHEAD, Surrogate, upon becoming pregna

embryo/fetus(s) until delivery. MARY BET

husband, agree that they will cooperate w

DDLING CLOTHES

, and Baby M, *by Judith Levine*

ry, 19**85**, by and between

s "Surrogate"), RICHARD WHITEHEAD,

RD STERN, (herein referred to as

llowing facts:

dual over the age of eighteen (18)

nable WILLIAM STERN and his

ted to WILLIAM STERN.

RD WHITEHEAD, her husband, are over

into this Agreement in consideration

promises contained herein and the

gree as follows:

s that she is capable of conceiving

hat in the best interest of the child,

lationship with any child or children

suant to the provisions of this

AM STERN, Natural Father, immediately

ghts to said child pursuant to this

HARD WHITEHEAD, her husband, have been

reement with the purposes, intents and

s wife, MARY BETH WHITEHEAD, Surrogate,

visions of this Agreement. RICHARD

ild, he will not form or attempt to form

en MARY BETH WHITEHEAD, Surrogate, may

ein, and agrees to freely and readily

STERN, Natural Father; and terminate his

dges he will do all acts necessary to

conceived and born pursuant to

ing blood testing and/or HLA testing.

hereby enter into this written contractual

re MARY BETH WHITEHEAD shall be

M STERN by a physician. MARY BETH

nowledges that she will carry said

HEAD, Surrogate, and RICHARD WHITEHEAD, her

background investigation into the

The agreement lies in a vague territory between contract law and family law—and neither seems sufficient to regulate it. Assume surrogate-parenting contracts are declared enforceable: how would the courts remedy a breach? If the mother backs out, will she be made to deliver the goods? If the father reneges and decides he doesn't want the child, should a judge force him to take the baby? In all this, the baby seems reduced to a commodity. What of his or her rights?

Richard Whitehead, a sanitation worker, makes $28,000. That's the family income; his wife, Mary Beth—the surrogate mother—is a homemaker. The Sterns, a biochemist and a pediatrician, have a joint income of more than $90,000. The class overtones of surrogate motherhood are creepy. Contracts are mainly between upper-middle-class couples and working-class (or lower-middle-class) women. There is the potential for exploitation: poor pay and awful working conditions for surrogate mothers. The contract called for Mary Beth Whitehead to make $10,000—about $1.50 an hour for 6,480 hours. And a father might try to control a surrogate mother's behavior: prohibit her from smoking, drinking, or having an abortion; or, in a difficult delivery, force her to undergo a Caesarean section. And what if a surrogate is sought for reasons other than the wife's inability to conceive? Couples could well turn to surrogates for eugenic purposes, with tall blond marathon runners and brilliant mathematicians demanding high prices.

The complications of surrogate motherhood have prompted twenty-seven state legislatures to propose laws regulating surrogacy, and several state courts have entered the fray. But in no state has a law been enacted. There have been other rulings: Catholic and Orthodox Jewish leaders have forbidden married couples to enter into surrogate arrangements, calling them adultery and a threat to the bonds of matrimony. Surrogate mothering, like pornography, is situated in that volatile zone where law and ethics, commerce and the body, intersect and widely divergent moralities collide. Lawmakers and judges cannot possibly foresee every problem. Yet they must begin to make some binding decisions. Families—especially children—can no longer afford to wait.

A SWEET DEAL

Price-fixing down on th

The Department of Agriculture each year regulates some $5.7 billion worth of fruits, vegetables, and "specialty crops" (hops, to name one) with "marketing orders." A total of forty-eight orders currently affect thirty-three different commodities. Some orders determine directly who may grow a crop, how much of it may be marketed, and in what form—say, fresh or frozen—it may be sold. There are also orders that stipulate the size and quality of produce that may be marketed—and thus *indirectly*, but quite effectively, control supply (and hence price). This is one such order, regulating the marketing of kiwifruit.

The Chinese gooseberry, as kiwifruit is known elsewhere in the world, grows on a twining vine. Native to south central China, it was introduced into New Zealand in 1906 (New Zealand soon became its principal producer) and into the United States in 1962 by Frieda Caplan, a Los Angeles broker of specialty produce. The fruit has furry greenish brown skin and a sweet taste, and in the late 1970s thin slices of it began to appear on nouvelle cuisine dishes. Kiwifruit sold in the United States (retail price ranges from thirty-five to sixty-nine cents apiece) is grown almost exclusively in California's Sacramento and San Joaquin valleys; last year's harvest was 4.3 million trays (each U.S. tray weighs seven pounds). Kiwifruit yields roughly $12,000 an acre, more than any other crop in the country—except marijuana.

The Department of Agriculture's Agricultural Marketing Service issues and enforces marketing orders. The federal government first got into the fruit and vegetable business in 1937 with the passage of the Agricultural Marketing Agreement Act (AMAA). Congress had tried to legalize price-fixing by farmers four years earlier, but the Supreme Court struck down the law. However, after Roosevelt's re-election in 1936, and his threat a year later to pack the Court, the justices reversed course; they began warming to greater government involvement. In this environment, the AMAA became law.

Doug Bandow worked for the Reagan administration as a special assistant to the president for policy development. He is now a senior fellow with the Cato Institute in Washington.

```
                              DEPARTMEN

                         Agricultural

                              7 CF

                         (Docket

KIWIFRUIT GR

                    Order Reg

    AGENCY:   Agricultural Marketing

    ACTION:   Final rule.

    SUMMARY:   This final rule establi

program to promote orderly marketing

order was favored by growers who prod

the production represented in a refer

by handlers representing more than the

shipments.   The program provides for

authority for grade, size, quality, ma

The program would be financed by asse

commodity.   The marketing order was c

1984.   The referendum was conducted b

September 10, 1984.




    EFFECTIVE DATE:   October 12, 1984

    FOR FURTHER INFORMATION CONTACT:

F&V, AMS, USDA, Washington, D. C. 2025
```

FOR KIWIFRUIT

arm, by Doug Bandow

GRICULTURE

ting Service

920

O 83-1)

CALIFORNIA

Handling

ce, USDA.

marketing agreement and order

ifornia kiwifruit. The marketing

ore than the required two-thirds of

The marketing agreement was signed

site 50 percent of total 1983-84

ittee for local administration and

y, pack, and container regulations.

s levied on handlers of the

red at a public hearing in February

Department by mail ballot August 31-

iam J. Doyle, Chief, Fruit Branch,

lephone (202-447-5975).

Marketing orders are supposed to ensure the "orderly marketing" of food products. In passing the AMAA, Congress hoped to lift farmers out of the Depression by limiting their output—thereby raising their profits to pre-World War I ("parity") levels. The all-important parity level for kiwifruit is determined by multiplying the average price over the previous ten years by the ratio of overall agricultural prices to costs between 1910 and 1914. If the market can't bring prices to this level, the government will attempt to do it by fiat—in this case, by ordering that an estimated 30 percent of all kiwifruit be kept from getting to market. This order bars farmers from selling fruit imperfect in shape or appearance (some pieces, for example, have blemished skin as a result of being "sunburned"). These imperfections have nothing to do with taste or nutrition. They have everything to do with creating artificially high prices, perhaps 30 to 40 percent higher than they would be without the order.

The regulatory process creates the illusion of public participation and farmer democracy. Actually, this order was preordained. After nine days of hearings last year—hearings that generated 2,018 pages of transcript—Agriculture Department officials could find no evidence of the sort of "acute economic emergency" Congress originally intended marketing orders to meet. Nevertheless, the White House, at the behest of a handful of the biggest of the 1,127 American kiwifruit farmers, instructed the department to issue the order. Even in voting on marketing-order referendums, the largest growers—with votes weighted according to crop size—have a disproportionately large say.

Although this marketing order, which went into effect last fall, was devised by and for the kiwifruit industry—the twelve-member Kiwi Administrative Committee established by the order has only one public representative—farmers everywhere can be heard loudly proclaiming their interest in the consumers' welfare. A more accurate testament to the farmers' sentiments is buried in a twenty-page Department of Agriculture notice printed last summer in the *Federal Register*. The notice says that the sale of "low grade" kiwifruit "will be likely to depress financial returns to growers."

The first atomic bomb, dropped on Hiroshima forty years ago, did not kill Akihiro Takahashi—nor did it spare him. The Japanese government has certified some 108,000 survivors of the blasts at Hiroshima and Nagasaki as *hibakusha*, or "explosion-affected persons"; this is Takahashi's official number. In accordance with the Law Pertaining to the Medical Treatment of Atomic Bomb Victims, passed in 1957 as a result of pressure brought by *hibakusha* organizations, certified survivors everywhere—there are about 750 living in the United States—are entitled to free medical care for bomb-related disabilities. Shown here are two pages from the registration booklet that Takahashi, like all *hibakusha*, must present to receive these benefits—a shorthand diary of his journey through the inferno.

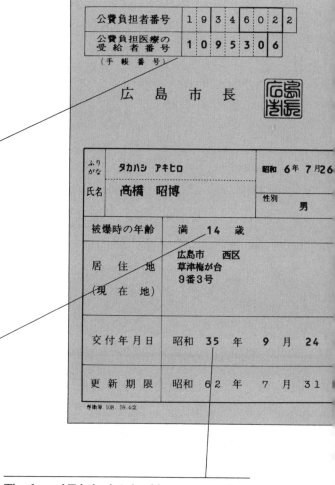

Takahashi was a fourteen-year-old schoolboy on August 6, 1945. A little after eight in the morning, as he and his sixty classmates were lining up for roll call, a friend pointed to a lone B-29 in the sky above Hiroshima. "Fall in," their teacher snapped, and as they did the world went dark and thunder engulfed them. The schoolyard was about a mile from ground zero. Five or ten minutes after the explosion, the heavy smoke faded away; when Takahashi came to his senses, he found he had been blown about thirty-five feet from where he had been standing. His clothes had burned away. From his hands and legs, the skin hung in sheets.

Robert Karl Manoff is a contributing editor of Harper's *and deputy director of the Center for War, Peace and the News Media at New York University.*

The first of Takahashi's booklets was issued on September 24, 1960; the date is recorded in *showa*, according to which the year is reckoned as the thirty-fifth in the reign of the Emperor Hirohito. To establish his eligibility, Takahashi had to prove that he had been in Hiroshima on the day of the bombing by providing corroboration from two witnesses—neither of whom, in accordance with the law, could be members of his family. Registration entitles him to semi-annual checkups and, should he need them, drugs, hospitalization, surgery, nursing care, and other medical treatment. Because he suffers from liver disease, one of eleven officially designated bomb-related conditions, he also receives an allowance of about $100 a week.

THE SURVIVOR

ime, *by Robert Karl Manoff*

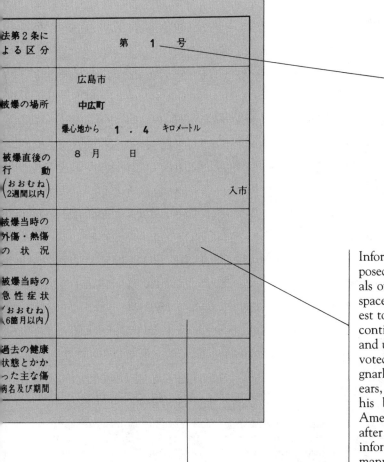

法第2条による区分	第　1　号		
被爆の場所	広島市 **中広町** 爆心地から **1 . 4** キロメートル		
被爆直後の行動 （おおむね 2週間以内）	8 月　　日		入市
被爆当時の外傷・熱傷の状況			
被爆当時の急性症状 （おおむね 6箇月以内）			
過去の健康状態とかかった主な傷病名及び期間			

The Medical Treatment law established four groups of victims. Takahashi is in the first (1), which includes those who were directly exposed to the bomb either in Hiroshima or Nagasaki. The second category includes those who came within a mile and a quarter of ground zero in the two weeks following the explosions. Those who went to the cities to help bury the dead and aid survivors make up the third category; those who were exposed to radiation *in utero*—mental retardation and other birth defects have been linked to prenatal exposure—make up the fourth group.

Information about Takahashi's injuries is supposed to be entered here. But after many renewals of the booklet, the officials now leave this space blank. History seems to be of little interest to the bureaucrats. But Takahashi, who has continued to live in Hiroshima (he is married, and until recently directed a museum there devoted to the bombing), cannot forget his badly gnarled right arm, his burned and shriveled ears, the thick scar tissue that encrusts parts of his body. Press censorship imposed by the American occupation forces during the years after the war effectively forbade publication of information about the bombings; as a result, many of those suffering from radiation sickness and other maladies believed they had contracted a rare contagious disease. Neighbors and friends, under the same impression, ostracized them.

Also left blank is the space for entering information about the subsequent onset of bomb-related illness. Medical studies of the survivor population organized by the U.S. government have shown dramatically higher levels of leukemia and of cancer of the lung, breast, stomach, and thyroid among *hibakusha*. Survivors (and their children) also face a continuing stigma and often encounter difficulties marrying and finding work. Because of this, and because of the stiff eligibility requirements, as many as 260,000 survivors—nearly as many people as have died as a result of the bombings—have not been officially designated. In a sense, they are being victimized a second time.

PAYING THE PIPER

The cost of culture

For ticket holders to the May 4 concert of the Cleveland Orchestra at Carnegie Hall, little was at stake save a pleasant evening in the company of Bach, Stravinsky, and Strauss. For the orchestra, however, the concert was an important appearance in the annual competition for attention on the historic Carnegie stage; its 106 musicians were there to satisfy the demands of corporate and government funders, individual donors, and music critics. For the hall, the evening was another in its "Great American Orchestras" series, one of a number of events it has organized since 1978, when it became an aggressive impresario. The hall would do better financially if it rented out space by the evening (at $3,700 during the week and $4,000 on weekends), as it did for its first seventy years, until 1961. But producing its own programs gives it greater control and allows it to "schedule more of the Cleveland Orchestra and the Juilliard String Quartet, and less of Rick Springfield," in the words of Seymour Rosen, the hall's artistic managing director. To this end, Carnegie produced 100 of the hall's 260 classical music events in the 1983–84 season, including concerts by thirty-four full-size and chamber orchestras. Such variety makes Carnegie the only hall in the world where, year after year, it is possible to judge which bands are hot and which are not.

George Szell, the music director of the Cleveland Orchestra from 1946 to 1970, used to say that an orchestra had to develop a regular New York showcase if it wanted to achieve greatness. In 1958, he launched an annual subscription series at Carnegie to show record company executives, agents, music publishers, critics, and fellow performers what he had built. Touring has become even more important since the Szell era. The current contract guarantees Cleveland musicians fifty-two paid weeks a year, which means that after the orchestra has saturated the Cleveland market (twenty-four weeks), played its summer season at the nearby Blossom Music Center (ten weeks) and its children's concerts (three weeks), and taken its vacation (eight weeks), it must go on tour for seven weeks to pay its bills. Critical success on the road assures contributors—who must make up the $3.3 million deficit in the orchestra's $16.4 million annual budget—that their money is being well spent. New audiences attracted by live performances on the tour help increase recording revenues, now $300,000 to $400,000 a year. Playing Carnegie is so important in these calculations that to introduce its new music director, Christoph von Dohnányi, the orchestra will increase the number of its appearances there next season from three to four.

This is a press seat. It is one of the reasons that Szell's New York strategy paid rich dividends in February 1963, when he was featured on *Time*'s cover as the magazine anointed Cleveland the leader of the big five U.S. orchestras (the others being the New York Philharmonic, Philadelphia, Boston, and Chicago). To quote *Time*: "The articulate clarity and precise balance that Szell has brought to the Cleveland give its performances a depth of detail and an intricacy that approach chamber music." In 1965, the orchestra was selected by the State Department to tour the Soviet Union, an event that earned it so much national attention that its concerts in Cleveland were completely sold out on subscription for the following season. Szell's yearly visits to Carnegie became major events. In 1970, the *New Yorker* even weighed in with a lengthy profile of the orchestra by Joseph Wechsberg. Szell died that same year, however, and his successor, Lorin Maazel, was unable to win the affection of the critics. Cleveland gradually lost its reputation as the hot band to Georg Solti and the Chicago Symphony. For this reason, the 1984–85 Carnegie appearances under von Dohnányi's baton will probably be the orchestra's most important in the last fifteen years. The critics will be listening closely; their verdict will shape the orchestra's fortunes both at home and on tour.

AT CARNEGIE HALL

by David M. Rubin

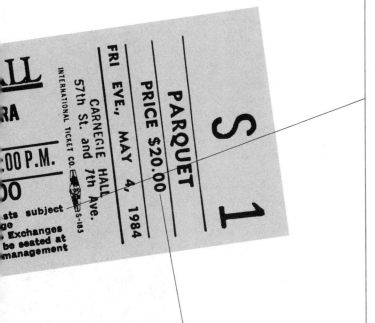

The hall was scaled from $12 to $20 for the 2,700 seats put on sale for this concert. Tickets were kept back for the press (fifty), for the orchestra manager and the conductor (a box of eight seats each), for the four soloists (four seats each), and for the house itself (Box 23 on the first tier). A few seats with obstructed views were also withheld. Given the average ticket price of $16, a Cleveland sellout would have produced about $43,000 for the Carnegie Hall Corporation. The principal expense incurred by the hall was the orchestra's fee of between $35,000 and $40,000 (which included the services of guest conductor Erich Leinsdorf). Rosen spent $9,900 to promote the event; he also had to pay the house staff and to account for general and administrative overhead for the hall. (The five stagehands, who often must work double shifts and dinnertime to get orchestras on and off the stage, each earn about $90,000 a year.) In all, the tab for this concert was between $60,000 and $65,000; the deficit was at least $20,000. Over the year, such losses accumulate to about $1.4 million in a budget of $11 million. Carnegie's directors approach foundations, corporations, Friends of the Hall, the New York State Council on the Arts, and the National Endowment for the Arts to close the gap. To make up the deficit through box office receipts alone, Carnegie would have to sell out concerts like these, night after night, at an average ticket price of at least $24.

The May 4 program was planned in the fall of 1982 by Leinsdorf, who had some juggling to do. First, he was scheduled to conduct both the Philadelphia Orchestra and the Philharmonic in New York during the same season, so he could not repeat anything on those programs. Second, because he and the orchestra's general manager, Kenneth Haas, had agreed to showcase four first-chair players as soloists, appropriate works had to be chosen. Third, the program had to have box office appeal. This meant avoiding most of the second Viennese school (Schönberg, Berg, and Webern) and their aesthetic heirs, as well as such fringe composers as Hummel. Finally, the program could run no more than the two and a half hours allowed under the musicians' contract. After consulting thirty index cards listing all of the orchestra's past New York programs, Leinsdorf chose a Bach concerto for violin and oboe, Strauss's *Don Quixote*, which features a cello and viola, and Dvořák's Symphonic Variations. When Rosen was informed of the program, his response was, "Too early, romantic, and romantic." He meant that the concerto would be played one year *before* Bach's 300th birthday celebration and that the Dvořák and Strauss were too similar in mood for a balanced program. But he was prepared to accede, as the program did not overlap with those already filed by other conductors in the series. Sometime later, however, while re-examining the score of the Dvořák, Leinsdorf remembered why he had avoided the piece over the years: he doesn't really like it. So he substituted Stravinsky's Symphony in Three Movements, a piece he calls "a shot of B-12 in the behind for the audience." Such changes occur all the time; this one came too late to be reflected in the first promotional brochures. Seymour Rosen knows he can sell out a performance by almost any orchestra with Beethoven's Ninth, the Verdi *Requiem*, or an all-Rachmaninoff program, but he tries to temper economic concerns with artistic ones. In February he permitted Michael Gielen and the Cincinnati Symphony to offer Alban Berg's Three Pieces for Orchestra, along with his Violin Concerto (on a program with two Schubert symphonies), hoping that the appearance of Yehudi Menuhin as soloist would override resistance to Berg. It didn't. The hall was only 72 percent filled. It was an experiment unlikely to be repeated. "Anyone who tours who says he doesn't consider box office," Leinsdorf declares, "either has no experience or is a liar."

David M. Rubin is the Dean of the S. I. Newhouse School of Public Communications at Syracuse University.

A (POST)MODERN (A

John Gotti: The substance

Last February 9, the jury in the Manhattan trial of John Gotti, the alleged chief of the Gambino crime family, found him not guilty of ordering the shooting of John O'Connor, leader of a union whose members had smashed up a Gambino restaurant because it had hired nonunion carpenters. This photo, taken at the trial, shows at least part of the explanation: John Gotti plays to the jury and to the wider audience with a constructed image, a *bella figura,* in his manner and his dress radiating goodwill and suggesting vicious retribution. Said the jury foreman afterward, "We're taken up by him, we're fascinated by the high life, the fast life." Said Michael Cherkasky, Gotti's prosecutor, of the verdict, "We had the evidence, but we didn't have the emotional appeal."

Every morning during the trial, a barber reportedly went to the modest Gotti house in the Howard Beach section of New York City to do a primping. Each bluish-gray streak was brushed back and up to make the entire head of hair perfect, arranged, untouchable—a head of stone, suggestive of control and power. He could butt your face with it. In 1973, in a Staten Island bar, Gotti and two others shot James McBratney in the head in retaliation for murdering a nephew of Carlo Gambino, the family's leader. After serving a brief two-year prison term for manslaughter, Gotti soared in the family chain of command. Now, assert law-enforcement officials, Gotti commands the largest crime family in the country—some 300 "made" members and 1,500 associates. Their business—drugs, gambling, loan-sharking, labor racketeering, etc.—grosses perhaps $500 million a year. The hair shows it all. Gotti is making myth of himself. He presents himself to jury and press as a human become statue, looming in stature, a temple god south of Rome somewhere.

Here is a man, suggests Gotti's amused eyes, whose intention is only to get unjust government off his back, as his defense attorney insists—only a plumbing-contracting salesman who makes no more than $60,000 a year. This is a message meant to appeal to the little people, the jurors of today and the jurors of tomorrow. And yet there may be another source of amusement for Gotti: In New York State, the court is required to give the names of the jurors to the defense. The jurors know this. They know too the tale about the Gotti neighbor who accidentally struck and killed Gotti's young son with his car. The neighbor has not been seen in ten years.

Marshall Blonsky is the editor of On Signs *(Johns Hopkins University Press) and the author of* American Mythologies *(Oxford University Press). He has taught semiotics at Vassar College and now does so at the New School for Social Research and Queens College.*

LLEGED) MOBSTER

is style, by Marshall Blonsky

The suit is custom-made by a tailor and costs about $1,800. The wide lapels italicize the chest, and the jacket is cut so close as to suggest that Gotti's massive thorax will crack through the armor. The members of the jury see this, of course. "A jury isn't supposed to be focused on the demeanor of a man who doesn't testify," said another of Gotti's former prosecutors, "but there was a feeling in the courtroom, a lot of things happening besides the words of the witnesses." During his trial for the O'Connor shooting, Gotti packed the courtroom with guys in sunglasses and gold chains. The power is not hidden. And below the suit, unseen here, are Gotti's leather shoes—soft, tassle-over-flap slip-ons that sell for $300. The effect is tasteful and leisurely; slipped over monogrammed socks, these are not the cheap slip-ons of a brawler, although in 1984 Gotti was brought to trial for assault and robbery of a refrigerator repairman who didn't recognize Gotti in a parking lot. But at the trial, the victim of Gotti's anger suddenly became incapable of identifying his assailant. Case dismissed.

The tie, the mark of a man's individuality, is flowered, effeminate in its bright colors, and thus Gotti is stating that he has so much surplus masculinity that he can appropriate the brilliant colors of femininity, as other men—the thin, pinched-looking prosecutors, for example—cannot. Notice too that the tie matches the shark-fin handkerchief. Usually, such an image suffices to command fear, but occasionally the testosterone has to be used, usually in an epic restaurant rubout: When Gotti grabbed the controls of the Gambino machine, it was to the eternal detriment of Paul ("Big Paul") Castellano, who was gunned down in front of Spark's Steak House in Manhattan during rush hour. Law-enforcement officials believe that Gotti is responsible for the murder. No charges have been brought so far.

The quintessential New York executive deflects attention to a fashion detail, the jacket that exactly shows the correct one half-inch of cuff. It's a style, a manner. Said the former head of the Justice Department's Organized Crime Strike Force, Edward McDonald: "If he had an education, he could be chairman of General Motors. He is an extraordinarily charming guy." That charm will be necessary again: In all likelihood another indictment is coming, this time on racketeering charges brought jointly by the Justice Department and the Manhattan district attorney, and so there should be more appearances by the dapper mobster. The press will eat it up. The jurors will think about the merits of the case, about their health, and about the man who sits before them. America needs its Gotti playing De Niro playing Capone for the Nineties. Don't expect the tailored don to spend any time behind bars soon.

THE TO[

Don't take Stanford's core list

It has been a busy spring at Bloom, Bellow & Bennett, the blue-chip firm of litigators in matters of civilization and constituted excellence. The case of *Stanford* v. *Western Culture* has grown to a bulging brief. The offense: firebrands on the Stanford University campus chanting "Hey hey, ho ho! Western Culture's got to go!" The students meant a required freshman course, its makeup, and not thousands of years of moral and intellectual reflection—and, in fact, late in March, the university did quietly decide to revise the course to make it more inclusive, less obviously ethnocentric. But the good men at B, B & B know an ambulance to chase when they see one. Bennett lamented the "faculty trashing of Shakespeare"; Bellow seemed to think the students would soon take to the trees, there to read "the Proust of the Papuans." But no one should take core-list revisions so seriously, because no one should take a core list seriously. The whole "core" idea is phony, if somewhat quaint, like a wealthy man's bookshelf of leather-bound, unopened classics.

"At least one Greek tragedy" seems decidedly minimal, no? Especially when you recall that the most famous Greek tragedy is a trilogy. This is a typical core-list strategy at Stanford and elsewhere: intellectual grazing. A little Genesis, a bit of Plato.

Is it essential to read Galileo, or *about* him? This seems a concession to the science faculty. A number of books seem to have made it onto the list as a result of the type of quota system B, B & B deem detestable. One imagines the meetings: medievalists, two required and one recommended; classicists, four and three; Comp Lit... meet you after class.

One hears much neo-con thundering about tokenism with regard to "core" matters, holding the line and all that. But tokenism is much in evidence already. The *Communist Manifesto* (1848) gives scant evidence of what eventually came from the pens of its authors in the field of political economy. But it does allow the mention of both Marx and Engels, lending the list a look of catholicity and fair play.

Christopher Hitchens is the Washington editor of Harper's Magazine.

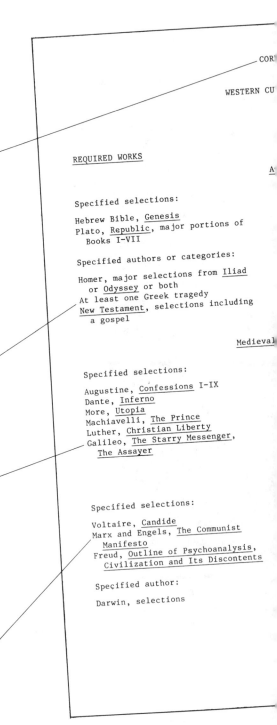

COR[

WESTERN CU

REQUIRED WORKS

A

Specified selections:

Hebrew Bible, Genesis
Plato, Republic, major portions of Books I-VII

Specified authors or categories:

Homer, major selections from Iliad or Odyssey or both
At least one Greek tragedy
New Testament, selections including a gospel

Medieval

Specified selections:

Augustine, Confessions I-IX
Dante, Inferno
More, Utopia
Machiavelli, The Prince
Luther, Christian Liberty
Galileo, The Starry Messenger, The Assayer

Specified selections:

Voltaire, Candide
Marx and Engels, The Communist Manifesto
Freud, Outline of Psychoanalysis, Civilization and Its Discontents

Specified author:

Darwin, selections

CANON

iously, *by Christopher Hitchens*

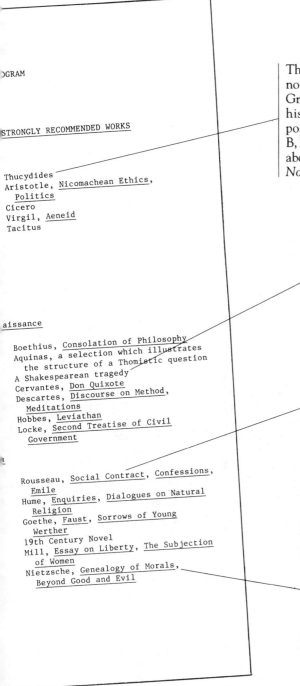

OGRAM

STRONGLY RECOMMENDED WORKS

Thucydides
Aristotle, <u>Nicomachean Ethics</u>,
    <u>Politics</u>
Cicero
Virgil, <u>Aeneid</u>
Tacitus

aissance

Boethius, <u>Consolation of Philosophy</u>
Aquinas, a selection which illustrates
    the structure of a Thomistic question
A Shakespearean tragedy
Cervantes, <u>Don Quixote</u>
Descartes, <u>Discourse on Method</u>,
    <u>Meditations</u>
Hobbes, <u>Leviathan</u>
Locke, <u>Second Treatise of Civil</u>
    <u>Government</u>

Rousseau, <u>Social Contract</u>, <u>Confessions</u>,
    <u>Emile</u>
Hume, <u>Enquiries</u>, <u>Dialogues on Natural</u>
    <u>Religion</u>
Goethe, <u>Faust</u>, <u>Sorrows of Young</u>
    <u>Werther</u>
19th Century Novel
Mill, <u>Essay on Liberty</u>, <u>The Subjection</u>
    <u>of Women</u>
Nietzsche, <u>Genealogy of Morals</u>,
    <u>Beyond Good and Evil</u>

Thucydides, Cicero, Tacitus—one sees here how the notion of Great Books, when "cored," gets reduced to Great Names. How should these authors be read—as history, politics, literature—and to what purpose? There is no sense of a battle for, or about, ideas. B, B & B shirk the combat of ideas, preferring to sneer about *The Color Purple* on all fours with *Le Rouge et le Noir.*

Who *gets* to Stanford without having read "a Shakespearean tragedy"?

Omissions abound—strange to have the French *philosophes* without even a sniff of countervailing Edmund Burke. Moreover, the books listed neatly under their headings give no sense that intelligent men and women disagree about which books belong in the canon. Karl Popper thought Hegel should be banned from the discourse; F. R. Leavis advised his students not to bother with Milton. Do any of the Bs imagine that this core list would have made sense to them (or anyone else) in 1950?

Nietzsche! The dreaded relativist on the core list? Look into it, Bloom. Of course, relativism arises not from Nietzsche—or Derrida or the Situationists—but from the use of arbitrary prefixes like "Western." If civilization means the sum of human intellectual accomplishment, it needn't be qualified by an adjective. (And if non-"Western" students want to claim North African analogues and antecedents for the classics, are they thereby not granting the premise of the classics' validity? What more could B, B & B ask?) Forget *core*—read deeply, widely, actively. I'm with Gandhi (who didn't make Stanford's list). When asked what he thought of Western civilization, he replied that it would be a very good idea.

THE SYSTEM THAT BRO

Zeroing in on a Pentagon boondoggle,

In the rush to judgment after the U.S. downing of Iran Air Flight 655, no guilty party was more carefully hidden in plain sight than Aegis, the high-tech radar system installed aboard the cruiser USS *Vincennes*. This most costly package of electronic complexity mistook an Airbus (length: 175 feet, 11 inches) for an F-14 (length: 62 feet, 8 inches), miscalculated the altitude of the plane by some 3,000 feet, and determined that the Airbus was descending when it was actually climbing (as can be gleaned from transcripts of radio calls between the jetliner and air controllers). So what is the problem with Aegis? As this letter displays, Aegis is simply the logical consequence of the present "defense" procurement system, dedicated to the simple principle: a bigger buck whatever the bang.

The "care" was mostly exerted to deceive Aegis's many critics. In one important series of tests, the Navy set up components of Aegis in a meadow near Exit 4 of the New Jersey Turnpike—"operational tests," the Navy called them. There Aegis performed such difficult tasks as monitoring the comings and goings of civilian air traffic over New York airports. As the Navy well knows, radar reflections off land are entirely different from those off water, and meadows don't pitch and roll—but then the object of the exercise was not any serious testing of Aegis but the extraction of more funds from Congress.

To counter missile attacks, ships such as the *Ticonderoga* and the *Vincennes* utilize the SLQ-32, an electronic system allied to Aegis that works like a Fuzzbuster—it identifies approaching ships and planes by the radar they emit. The SLQ-32 on the *Vincennes*, however, was unable to distinguish between the weather radar aboard an Airbus and the combat radar installed in an F-14.

Alexander Cockburn is a columnist for The Nation *and the* Los Angeles Times. *Ken Silverstein is a journalist based in Rio de Janeiro.*

THE SECRE
WASHING

The Honorable Denny Smith
House of Representatives
Washington, D.C. 20515

Dear Mr. Smith:

I am responding to your
questioned the integrity of th
of operational testing of USS

Reports of inadequate tes
system are not correct. AEGIS
combat system ever built. Pri
we completed over 100,000 hour
three sea trials. Extensive o
since commissioning and all op
met or exceeded.

TICONDEROGA establishes a
anti-air warfare capability --
to counter large scale anti-sh
fast reaction time and high fi
have proven successful in coun
testing against the lowest fly
to the Fleet. TICONDEROGA, ac
forces, provides a quantum lea
capability of our carrier batt

TICONDEROGA's success in
affirms our full confidence in
The capability TICONDEROGA pro
in the world. Further product
ship's performance.

I appreciate your support

Sin

Joh

UGHT DOWN FLIGHT 655

/ Alexander Cockburn and Ken Silverstein

OF THE NAVY
).C. 20350

11 October 1983

. letter in which you
JIS system and the results
NDEROGA (CG-47).

of TICONDEROGA and its AEGIS
.he most carefully tested
) TICONDEROGA's commissioning,
successful testing, including
.ional testing has continued
.onal requirements have been

.irely new level of sea-borne
.s the first Navy ship designed
.ssile (ASM) attacks. The
.ver of the AEGIS weapon system
.g ASM threats in operational
.nd fastest targets available
.in concert with other battle
.ward in the defense in depth
.oups.

.t battle group exercises
. ship and its AEGIS system.
. is unmatched by any ship
.s entirely justified by the

. strong Navy.

.y,

.man

Representative Denny Smith, Republican from Oregon, forced a new round of tests of Aegis in May 1984 after actual sea tests a year earlier impressed no one but the Navy and RCA, the prime contractor. In these new tests, Aegis performed marvelously, "downing" ten of eleven drones sent its way. It was aided in this enterprise by the fact that those operating the system already knew the path and speed of the drones making up the "surprise" attack.

Nonsense. Aegis is particularly inept at detecting planes and missiles at low altitude, the most likely path of any aggressor. In two 1983 tests, Aegis missed six of seven low-altitude targets.

Aegis in fact imperils every ship on which it is installed. The system emits four megawatts of energy—equivalent to 40,000 100-watt light bulbs—the moment it is activated, turning the ship into a powerful electronic beacon and making it an easy target, especially for the radar-homing missiles the Soviets have sensibly developed.

Support indeed—each Aegis costs the taxpayers about $500 million, half the cost of the cruiser on which it is installed.

John Lehman—who as Secretary of the Navy was the patron and close friend of Melvyn Paisley, the key figure in the current procurement scandal under FBI investigation—thought the expense of the Aegis system "entirely justified." Admiral Thomas Davies, who before retiring tried to kill the program, calls the system "the greatest expenditure to get the least result in history"—which should be adopted as the motto of today's military procurement system. A pair of binoculars could have told the officers of the *Vincennes* what was flying overhead. But binoculars don't cost half a billion dollars. The more complex the weaponry, the deeper the pork barrel and the more swollen the bottom line. This is the system that produced Aegis, and did in the 290 passengers aboard Flight 655.

Counterfeiting a Federal Reserve note is a fine art and a felony. Title 18, Section 504, of the federal criminal statutes actually forbids newspapers and magazines from reproducing images of dollar bills unless they accompany a "newsworthy" story. What is news just now is that the illegal printing of paper money is on the rise, and officials fear that this renaissance of counterfeiting has yet to reach full flower. The Secret Service, chartered in 1865 specifically to combat counterfeiting, uncovered 115 printing operations in 1983, the most ever, and 34 percent more than in 1982. Agents seized $63,959,780 in phony bills (mostly $20s and $50s) before they could be passed along. About $8 million worth of forged money is believed to be in circulation. A bit of perspective: though counterfeiting is increasing, the problem is nothing compared with what it was in 1865, when money was printed by banks, not the government. The portion of money then in circulation thought to be counterfeit was one third.

More and more counterfeiting of American dollars is done overseas—Colombia is the largest foreign "manufacturer." The Secret Service suspects that there are links between counterfeiting and drug trafficking. Another explanation for the increase in overseas counterfeiting might be the lack of raw materials here: it is illegal in the United States to make paper similar to that used by the Bureau of Engraving and Printing. The bureau will not disclose the formula for the paper, nor will the paper's manufacturer, Crane and Company, of Dalton, Massachusetts. Currency was once 100 percent linen; now it is a cotton-linen blend. The red and blue fibers, once silk, are now nylon.

Experts say that one of the toughest things to forge is the engraved portrait of George Washington. G. F. C. Smillie did the engraving, and it has been on the dollar bill since 1918. Smillie copied his work from Gilbert Stuart's "Athenaeum" portrait of 1796, now in the Museum of Fine Arts in Boston. Stuart had sought a more animated expression from Washington, but could not get him to talk: he had just had a set of false teeth inserted. But it is not the tight lips that counterfeiters botch; it is Washington's soft, somewhat melancholy stare.

NDLING CURRENCY

ght, by William Poundstone

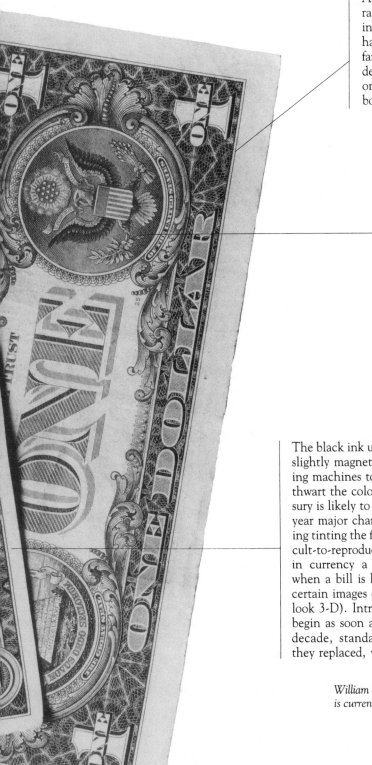

The Treasury denies that the artwork on American currency is anything more than decorative. But the Bureau of Engraving and Printing periodically receives calls from people who have "discovered" secret signs and codes. Most famous, perhaps, is the three-millimeter "spider" that *appears* to appear here, on the border on the back of the bill. See it? The roundish body and four crablike legs?

Forming the backdrop to the Great Seal is a pattern of fine parallel lines, crosshatched at the top and bottom of the circle to create a chiaroscuro effect. The lines and crosshatching are executed with a parallel-ruling machine capable of microscopic exactitude. Such minute detail has long been the main line of defense against counterfeiting. But a new era is in the offing. Battelle Laboratories recently studied the forgery problem for the Federal Reserve. Information turned up by this study has led officials to fear that there will be a surge of "amateur" counterfeiting by the end of the decade. The cause of this panic is the development of a new-technology color copier; it may soon be sophisticated enough to quickly, easily, and cheaply reproduce currency engraving. Researchers think that there will be 1,000 to 2,000 color copiers in private hands by 1990—and that not all those hands will be clean.

The black ink used on the front of dollar bills is slightly magnetic—just enough for bill changing machines to detect photocopy phonies. To thwart the color-copy counterfeiters, the Treasury is likely to announce before the end of the year major changes in currency. It is considering tinting the front margins of bills with a difficult-to-reproduce mix of pastel colors; inserting in currency a "security thread" visible only when a bill is held up to a light; or replacing certain images on bills with holograms (which look 3-D). Introduction of the new bills could begin as soon as next year. By the end of the decade, standard greenbacks, like the coins they replaced, will be history.

William Poundstone is the author, most recently, of The Ultimate. *He is currently writing a book on John von Neumann and game theory.*

AN IMAGE OF A
Food for everything but

Help yourself to a fine crystal flute of cold brut champagne and raise it to the imaginative men and women, the "food stylists," who spend as long as a week to create photographs like this—photographs of *interesting* meals, *creative* meals, meals that you too might prepare or might eat at just the right restaurant, meals that say something about you. You have seen so many of these pictures: in magazines devoted to food, in commercials and glossy advertisements, more often than not bathed in the kind of golden light (like here) that makes you feel warm, the way you feel when you share good food with good friends at those special times. So lift your glass of bubbly . . . but don't drink it. Don't *ruin* everything. The champagne shown here is actually ginger ale—soda holds its bubbles longer and *looks* so much more real. And to make the ginger ale look the way you most desire champagne to look—so fizzy you can feel the tickle on your tongue—the food stylist has tossed in a helping of salt.

Fresh ice cream, made with your very own ice-cream maker—that one you saw in the catalogue pictured with a dish of *rich, creamy* ice cream and, right then, knew you needed. Ice cream always looks so *tempting* when you see it in pictures. In ads for ice cream, the peach ice cream has so many bits of peach, the chocolate chip so many chocolate chips. This is because imaginative food stylists have the care and patience to pick every last chocolate chip out of a gallon of the chocolate chip ice cream they are tempting you with and put them all into those one or two scoops you see—thereby technically complying with truth-in-advertising laws that state that the food shown in an ad must be the food being advertised. If a photo is not for an ad, no such laws apply, so stylists can really *create:* The super-creamy "ice cream" here is actually Crisco vegetable shortening, whipped in a Cuisinart with red food coloring and a few red cherries, then molded to look just the way you like it.

These are, in fact, cherries. Really. They're "heroes," as the stylists say, perfect specimens. They are what previous pictures have taught you to look for in a cherry. In this case, two heroes could not be found with stems attached, which is how you want them to look when you want them to say "fresh." The stylist had to glue the best stems he could find to two cherries. The cherries were then coated with olive oil to add a healthy, natural sheen.

Photograph by Rick Mariani. Styling by Robert Skotnicki

PETITE APPEASED

ing, *by Tom Thompson*

Look! Someone has poured the espresso. You didn't see the coffee being poured, because pouring is very hard for the stylist to get just right. Wine especially, when being poured, looks wrong, not as silky and magnificent as we expect—*demand*—wine to look. Stylists substitute a syrupy concoction made of glycerine and Welch's grape juice, which pours the way we think wine should pour. (The perfectionist can even go one step further: A New York company called Trengove makes acrylic carvings of wines in mid-pour.) Coffee's problem, pouring aside, is a tendency to develop an oily residue on its surface during the hours of styling and photographing. Needed was something that looks like coffee in a picture. What you have here is a cup of room-temperature molasses.

Our main dish, the game hen—Mediterranean, in keeping with our *mood:* Look at the fresh rosemary!—is (like those shrimp) virtually raw. Nonetheless, the hen took *time:* First, the skin was pinned down at the back to remove unsightly wrinkles. The bird was then cooked for fifteen minutes at about 500 degrees, for a nice, crispy, home-cooked look. Finally, the food stylist alternated between brushing the hen with an oleaginous mixture of water and Kitchen Bouquet—a "browning product"—and drying it off with a hand-held blow-dryer, until a juicy shine appeared. Ten or twelve coats and it was ready for the table. Of course, should the color later seem somehow *unnatural*, the skin can be made to look even fresher and crispier with Scitex, the computerized photo-enhancing system. Nothing is real for those wanting nothing but the best.

Shrimp and pasta? A splendid choice—very now, very Mediterranean, and very, very carefully prepared. It took the food stylist hours to find the perfect bunch of basil to yield two perfectly green-looking, fresh-looking, basil-looking leaves like these. Then an assistant on the crew properly boiled the pasta for about thirty seconds, leaving it raw and hard—just right for arranging. Finally, using a heating filament removed from a toaster oven, the food stylist took shrimp cooked only enough to turn them pink and painstakingly applied to each of them three perfectly spaced "grill marks."

Tom Thompson is a free-lance writer living in San Francisco.

Playing on the pipe of racial fear and jealousy, the Murdoch press appeals whenever possible to the prejudices of any ethnic faction large enough to elect a politician or stage a parade. In New York and Boston the papers pay court to the Irish; the *Boston Herald* has gone so far as to run a story praising the heroes of the IRA. In London, of course, the Murdoch press associates the Irish with terrorism, anarchy, and the Third World.

One of the many corporate entities that constitute Rupert Murdoch's press holdings. In addition to holding a substantial interest in Reuters, Murdoch controls twenty-eight operating companies in Britain, among them the *Times* papers, the *Sun*, and the *News of the World*; ten publications in the United States, among them the *New York Post*, the *Boston Herald*, the *Village Voice*, the *Chicago Sun-Times*, the *Star*, the *San Antonio Express*, and *New York* magazine; and fifty-one operating companies in Australia, including twenty-seven newspapers and a television network. Most of his editors diligently study and obediently observe the typology of the lurid. The *Sun*, probably the crudest of the Murdoch papers, earned more than $30 million last year; the *Star*, a weekly tabloid sold in American supermarkets, earned $14 million. These two publications provide the profits that allow Murdoch to operate the London *Times* papers at an annual loss of $11 million and the *New York Post* at an annual loss of $14 million. The *Star* enjoys the distinction of having once conducted an interview with Jesus Christ.

The Murdoch press is on familiar terms with the big people, the godlike figures who hold the world in their hands, the people who count. Mondale is "Fritz," Reagan is "Ron," and New York City Mayor Koch is "Ed." These friendly and honorific forms of address pertain only to benign deities. Evil spirits (i.e., liberals, commies, homosexuals) retain their formal names. Senator Gary Hart is "Hart," not "Gary."

Harold Evans is the president and publisher of the adult trade division of Random House, Inc. He is also the founder of Condé Nast Traveler.

OF THE LURID

into an urban fairy tale, *by Harold Evans*

The Murdoch press is the stuff that dreams are made on, and none more seductive than the dream of wealth. Nobody wins big enough to buy a yacht, much less a line of horses or dancing girls, but the papers do their best to conceal the bad news that on a reader's lucky, lucky day he will be lucky to win $25 and a bored smile from a clerk in the circulation department. In Boston, New York, and Chicago the Murdoch tabloids promote their lotteries as if they were contests of skill, but the schemes test little more than the reader's capacity to buy the paper and count to ten.

Like most everything else in the paper, a half-truth. The *Post* cannot claim the largest sale; it sells 960,000 copies a day, as opposed to 1.4 million copies sold by the New York *Daily News*. Nor is the *Post*'s circulation increasing as rapidly as *USA Today*'s, which didn't exist when Murdoch acquired the *Post* in 1976 and gave it a motto. The line about its dizzying growth is meant to frighten the *Daily News*, and has forced that paper to keep its price down and to waste its substance on promotion. The apt comparison is to a game of blindman's bluff or an arms race between African despots.

Shouting sans-serif headlines, of crude cut and emotive wording, dominate what the trade calls a "circus layout." The jigsaw pattern seeks to convey the impression that everything happened at once, which is appropriately miraculous but sometimes disconcerting. Is the man in the photograph the crazed mental patient? No, he is the future archbishop of New York. But for a single, glorious moment the reader might wonder if a priest had run amok with a knife instead of a box of socks. The intention is to jostle, distract, and entertain, to say to the reader, Move on, read this, look at that. The line "Mental Patient Stalked Reagan" isn't bad. "Mental patient" perhaps isn't as good as "psychopath" or "madman," but "stalked" certainly is better than "traipsed after." Best would have been "Ape-Mother Steals Kennedy Child." But in the Murdoch press, thieving ape-mothers appear only once or twice a year, usually in the *Star*, and, for reasons not yet adequately understood, usually prefer to steal children in California or Texas.

President Reagan's magnificence is a common-place of the Murdoch press. Possibly as an act of devotion to its new owner, the *Chicago Sun-Times* last May went so far as to fit Mr. Reagan for a crown. A variation of the text undoubtedly will appear in the *New York Post* in late October, possibly with a newly discovered connection to Charles V or Louis XIV. Because Mr. Reagan rules by divine right, it is not inconceivable that if the campaign goes badly for him, and if good old Fritz Mondale shows an insolent commoner's strength in the public opinion polls, one of the Murdoch papers will print a story about the raising of a man from the dead in the White House Rose Garden.

Fear is rival only to greed among the emotions exploited by the Murdoch press. The papers present a kind of Grand Guignol in which gangsters, together with Soviet generals, play the role of principal villain. The facts are always sketchy and never very important. Of the thirteen mobsters arrested for various crimes, the *Post* names only four. It is enough that the apparitions of nightmare wear only the most conventional masks and costumes. The typology of the lurid requires the arrangement of sensational crimes into a strict hierarchy. Illicit sex always enjoys a preferred place, unless, of course, it occurs between members of minority groups or among people too poor to shop at Bloomingdale's. Murder stands somewhat higher in rank (again with the proviso that the deceased is somebody prominent in East Hampton or Mafia circles); murder combined with illicit sex stands almost on a footing with the crimes and misdemeanors committed by movie stars and princes of the realm. Given a perfect set of circumstances, the headline would read, "Call-Girl Wife Feeds Millionaire Hubby to Sharks."

Ronald Reagan *President*

John F. Kennedy *President*

Mary Stuart *Queen of Scots*

King Carl XVI Gustaf *Sweden*

Beatrix *Queen of Netherlands*

A REAGAN COU

From Sun-Times Wires
LONDON—President Reagan, descended from Ireland's most famous warrior-king, is related to nine of Europe's ruling monarchs, the president of France and even the late President John F. Kennedy, the renowned genealogical firm Burke's Peerage said yesterday.

In fact, Reagan is the most "royal" U.S. president since George Washington, who was closely related to Britain's royalty, said Burke's director, old Brooks-Baker.

there was a m could, according

dictum, bring peace to the world through his cousins, it's Ronald Reagan."

The common link is the greatest of Irish kings, Brian Boru, who saved his country from the Vikings in the 11th century. Most European royalty is descended from him through Mary Queen of Scots, and Reagan also is a direct descendant.

Burke's said Reagan's ... which goes ... years.

een, from grandfathe grated dur tato famin

Reagan, the Burke' in Peking has been royal line long have gan's roya Peskett, nealogist, Sherlock tor trac years ch

RK POST, WEDNESDAY, MARCH 28, 1984

DA IND IN MO

By MIKE PEARL and JAMES NORMAN
THIRTEEN men, including several top mobsters, were arrested today and accused of stonewalling a Manhattan grand jury investigating loan sharking and extortion.

Manhattan DA Robert Morgenthau said the 13 included Joseph Yacovelli, who authorities in the past have said they believe is the mobster that ordered the 1972 murder of mob chief Joseph Gallo.

The DA said that eva-

sive answers and refu to answer questions h hampered efforts to " velop certain evidence prosecute a number people."

Morgenthau didn't sa who the ultimate target of the probe were, but was clear from cour papers that they in cluded Matthew (Matty the Horse) Ianiello and John (Buster) Ardito.

The DA said the grand jury was trying to determine the leaders and members of criminal groups operating a multimillion-dollar loan-

Body of mi found

A BLOATED body that had been in the Hudson River for seven weeks was identified yesterday as the missing Mahopac man who disappeared after killing his wife and her young lover.

"We just received fingerprints and the ID matches Thomas Milligan. We are positive," said Yonkers Police Capt. Owen McClain.

THOMAS MILLIGAN *Double murderer.*

rters ing.

Photo

| Margreth II
Queen of
Denmark | Baudouin
King of
Belgium | Franz II
Liechten-
stein | Grand Duke
Jean
Luxembourg | Francois
Mitterrand
France | Princess
Diana
England |

...IN IN EVERY PALACE

England, makes Reagan related to Britain's Queen Elizabeth II and the ruling monarchs in Spain, Norway, Sweden, Denmark, the Netherlands, Belgium, Luxembourg and Lichtenstein.

He also is related to the dethroned royalty of Russia, Italy, Austria, Greece, Romania and Bulgaria. About the only ones he is not kin to are the Grimaldis of Monaco.

Peskett first traced Reagan's Irish roots in 1980. He has said the forebears ...tic presidential ...

dale were Vikings, "and Brian Boru always beat the Vikings."

"By finding this document, we have been able to prove beyond any shadow of a doubt that the Reagans were royal," Brooks-Baker said.

The Reagans are descended from Boru's brother Donnchuan through his son, Riagain (the Reagan name has undergone various spelling changes over the centuries). Riagain's younger brother, Ceinneitich, is an ancestor of the Kennedy family.

French President Francois Mitterrand is descended from Boru on the female side and thus is a cousin of Reagan, who descended on the male side.

The Riagains were minor kings with a small kingdom in the Fermoy area near Cork. But Peskett said they eventually were dispossessed and reduced from kings to peasants by the ancestors of the present princess of Wales.

Peskett figures Reagan and Princess Diana, wife of Prince Charles, are 28th cousins.

CTS 13
PROBE

...king, gambling and ...rtion ring.

...x of the 13 men who ...e arrested this morn... had refused to an... any questions after ...were sworn in, Mor...au said.

...ther six allegedly ..."evasive, equivocal ...onspicuously unbe... ...le answers."

...13th declined to ...he would tell the ...Morgenthau said. ...rding to the crimi... ...ontempt indict... ...against the men, ...li, 56, had ...questions con...

cerning conversations picked up by electronic bugs about loans.

Another of the arrested men, Nicholas (Nicky the Blond) Frustaci, 52, was charged with giving "patently false" answers to whether he had ever discussed owing Ianiello $100,000.

He also had been asked whether he was party to discussing a plan to set on fire a supermarket in Queens or whether he told officials at the market the mob "didn't kill people for money but only does that for rats."

...ing killer
...n Hudson

... as the police ...rned the case is

...ly was found ...floating 100 ...the Yonkers ...r the JFK

...re no signs of ...d gun wounds ...uries.

...46, had been ...nce Feb. 1, ...led his ea-

...tranged wife, Annette, 38, and her lover, Kenneth Anderson, 20, of Bedford, in the master bedroom of his home.

About an hour after the killings, a car rented to Milligan was found on the Tappan Zee Bridge with its motor running.

Milligan's wallet was found on the front seat, along with a sales slip for a shotgun he had bought one day earlier in Port Chester.

No one saw ...

The Murdoch phantasmagoria requires all accused to be, by definition, blood-red guilty. In this instance, the accused is conveniently dead and thus beyond the guile of a greedy lawyer who might persuade him to press a complaint of libel. The story can take the form of a fairy tale. It meets the specifications of suburban nightmare (thereby preserving the Manichaean division of the world into the hell of Mahopac, New York, and the heaven on the other side of Wingo). Judging by his photograph, Mr. Thomas Milligan probably never lived in a $12,000 trailer, much less a $100,000 house, but, as has been said, the blessing of money redeems even the most sordid crime from the commonplace realm of domestic discontent. The routine debasement of language in the Murdoch press means that words must either be deployed as weapons or traded as the cheap currency of pulp fiction. Mr. Milligan's body is necessarily "bloated," his features "distorted." The same vocabulary of violence carries over into the sports pages, where games cannot be distinguished from homicides. Players do not defeat one another; they get blitzed, blasted, clawed, ripped, buried, demolished, gunned down. In the Murdoch press, a stadium is an abattoir.

BETTING TOO B

The thoroughbred breeding bul

This colt, referred to simply as Hip No. 173—that's the number pasted on the horse's rump—was one of 256 yearlings auctioned last July at the annual Keeneland Selected Yearling Sale, the most prestigious thoroughbred auction in the world. It's a two-day sale, held in a pavilion adjacent to the Keeneland racetrack in Lexington, Kentucky. The catalogue for the sale is as arcane as any from Sotheby's, and as full of rare and expensive treasures. The yearlings auctioned at Keeneland in 1986 went for a total of $104.4 million, with eighteen of the young horses bringing a million dollars or more. Hip No. 173 was purchased for $1.85 million; in recent years, breeding, not racing, has been the action in thoroughbreds.

Hip No. 173's sire, Nijinsky II, was purchased in 1968 for $84,000 by Charles Engelhard. The horse won $677,118 in purses during his racing career in Europe, and in 1970 was named European Horse of the Year. But his racing career would be a brief one: by the early 1970s it was clear to owners that a champion could make more money in the breeding shed than on the track. In August 1970 Nijinsky II was syndicated, and brought back to Lexington to do stud duty at Claiborne Farm. The syndication price was $5.4 million, a record at the time, but the horse has since earned that and much, much more. In 1986, the rights to a single spurt of the stallion's semen brought $425,000, and for good reason: he has sired ten champions and more than a hundred stakes winners. Two years ago, a son of Nijinsky II, out of the dam of Seattle Slew, brought a record bid of $13.1 million.

Kentucky—with its limestone-rich soil and its fine grass—has been the center of thoroughbred breeding since the late nineteenth century. Certain farms have tended to dominate racing, because champions tend to beget champions. The ancestry of Colt 173's dam, Christmas Bonus, is intertwined with the three great Bluegrass dynasties of the past forty years. Four generations back is the stallion Bull Lea, who became the foundation sire of the great (in the forties and fifties) Calumet Farm. Two generations back is Bold Ruler, who enabled the Phipps family to dominate racing in the 1960s. Three generations back is the Claiborne Farm stallion Nasrullah, one of the genetic fonts of racing today.

G ON THE BLOOD

, boom to burst, *by Carol Flake*

d Farm

	Hip No.
	173

ssing H.). Second dam SUGAR
Yule Log (dam of CHRISTMAS
o Sweet Tooth (stakes-placed,
'DAR; etc.).

985

```
rn Dancer ......┌Nearctic
              └Natalma
              ┌Bull Page
ng Page .........└Flaring Top
              ┌Graustark
o the Mint .......└Key Bridge
              ┌Bold Ruler
ar Plum Time .....└Plum Cake
```

e year. Among the leading sires in
ners, including champions Golden
nd Ireland, Epsom Derby-**G1**, etc.),
and), Caerleon (French Derby-**G1**,
Derby-**G1**, etc.), Solford (champion
nd), Princesse Lida (in France, Prix
n).

wins, 3 to 5, $140,557, Poquessing H.
a 2-year-old of 1986.

at 3 and 4, $198,856, Firenze H.-**G2**,
on H.-**G2**, 3rd Ladies H.-**G1**, Sheridan
inners, incl.—
Mint). Stakes winner, above.

43,901, Jasmine S., etc. Half-sister to
Dam of 8 winners, including—
e S., National Stallion S., etc.
, 2nd Alcibiades S. Broodmare of the
ace, 7 winners, including—
mpion 3-year-old filly, C.C.A. Oaks-**G1**,
, Fantasy S.-**G2**, etc.
4, $957,195, Florida Derby-**G1**, Cham-
ue Grass S.-**G1**, etc. Sire.
and 3, $257,046, Mother Goose S.-**G1**,
RE TURN (to 3, 1986, $53,020).
3rd Peter Pan S.-**G2**.
foals to race, all winners, including—
starts at 3 and 4, $563,670, champion 3-
Ruffian H.-**G1**, Gulfstream Park H.-**G1**,
iss S.-**G3**, etc.
PRUNEPLUM ($191,456). Granddam of
Forbes [L] (at 2, 1985, $62,110).

gton-Washington F., Kentucky Jockey

What came to be known as the Bluegrass breeding bubble can be traced back to Northern Dancer, sire of Nijinsky II. Ever since Irish trainer Vincent O'Brien proved with a son of Northern Dancer named The Minstrel that Nijinsky's feat had been no fluke, that American horses could win big European races, big money has chased after the Dancer's offspring. In the mid-1970s, the yearling market was dominated by Greek shipping magnates. The Greeks were followed by Robert Sangster, heir to the Liverpool-based Vernons' soccer-pool fortune. In 1982 Sangster joined with Stavros Niarchos and others to buy a colt by Nijinsky II for $4.25 million, a record at the time.

Sons of Nijinsky II, and sons of other horses sired by Northern Dancer, have become champions around the world. The Japanese chased after colts in the Dancer line at Keeneland; more recently, it has been the Arabs—in particular, the three sons of the prime minister of the oil-rich United Arab Emirates: Mohammed, Hamdan, and Maktoum al Maktoum. This has made for great drama at Keeneland: Europeans banding together to bid against Arabs, Arabs refusing to be outbid, records falling each summer—$4.25 million in 1982, $10.2 million in 1983...But the high prices were making owners feel it was too dangerous to keep their horses running—an injury could ruin a future stud career. The quality of horses racing on American tracks lessened as owners retired their horses: in 1986, only two of the best three-year-olds of '85 were still racing. As a result, attendance at some tracks has fallen off.

The Breeders' Cup is the Super Bowl of racing, designed to provide new racetrack incentives for owners and breeders and to rebuild an audience for a sport that has come to be deprived too soon of its stars. But last year's Keeneland sale may have offered a more crucial incentive: the market. The average price for a yearling dropped 24 percent from the 1985 average. For the first time in recent years, the average price nationwide of a Northern Dancer colt fell below a million dollars. When the prices for good horses get low enough, owners will be more inclined to forgo the early trip to the breeding shed, and to keep their champions where they belong—on the track.

Carol Flake is the author of two books on horse racing, Tarnished Crown (Doubleday) *and* Thoroughbred Kingdom (Bullfinch).

THE BOOK O

The 'pass' and the power

This is the reference book, or pass, carried by Temba, as I shall call him. All Africans in South Africa must register for a pass at sixteen. When Temba was issued his (he is now thirty-eight), he was ordered to carry it with him twenty-four hours a day and to produce it whenever a police officer demanded. To do otherwise could mean a fine or even jail. Police "pass raids" are frequent; every two minutes an African is arrested on a pass-related offense. Current laws requiring Africans to carry passes—whites do not carry them, nor do the country's 3.6 million mixed-descent "Coloureds" and Asians—date from the 1950s. They underpin apartheid. In South Africa, the government of a white minority (4.7 million people) controls an African majority (22.7 million). The pass is an instrument of that control.

Temba's residential address is listed in Section A as Evaton—an African township south of Johannesburg. Johannesburg and its environs are part of the 87 percent of South Africa officially designated "white." Here, only whites may buy land or establish permanent residence. An African can qualify for quasi-residential status in a white area if he was born in such an area and has lived there continuously, or if he has worked in a white area for the same employer for ten years continuously (or for more than one employer for fifteen years continuously). All other Africans are allowed into white areas only to work, and may live there in the segregated townships only as long as they have a proper work permit in their passes.

In Section H, Temba is classified as "Zulu"; the space for citizenship is left blank. The government considers Temba not a citizen of South Africa but rather a citizen of KwaZulu, one of the ten "homelands" established for Africans by the government; since 1976, it has been pressuring the "homelands" to become "independent." KwaZulu is not a single, contiguous area but an archipelago of territories in the Natal province. Zulus oppose its "independence," demanding South African citizenship instead. KwaZulu has little arable land. There is no gold, no diamonds. Here, Temba has been told, he can exercise the political rights denied him in the land of his birth.

Stephanie Urdang is a journalist and the author of And Still They Dance: Women, War, and the Struggle for Change in Mozambique, *published by Monthly Review Press.*

APARTHEID

e text, *by Stephanie Urdang*

Afrikaans is one of two official languages in South Africa (English is the other); no African language is so recognized. The country's 2.7 million Afrikaners are descendants of seventeenth-century Dutch, German, and Huguenot settlers. In 1948, the Afrikaner-dominated National Party came to power, ending years of rule by the pro-British United Party. (South Africa withdrew from the Commonwealth in 1961.) National Party rule brought about an intensification of discriminatory and repressive legislation: the Population Registration Act and the Group Areas Act, both passed in 1950; the Reservation of Separate Amenities Act, passed in 1953.

Temba's tax payments are recorded in the pages of Section C (and Section D). The average white makes four and a half times as much as the average black. And yet the rare African family of four earning R6,000 a year (about $3,000) will pay twice as much tax as a four-member white family earning the same amount. And what can an African expect for his tax rand? *Education*: the government spends R192 each year for an African student (R1,385 for a white). *Pensions*: the government spends R65 a month for an African (R166 a month for a white). *Health Care*: 30 to 50 percent of African children die before their fifth birthday.

Few Africans are granted licenses to carry arms. In 1983, 1,794,289 licenses were issued, 4.7 percent to Africans. Half of all white South Africans own small arms, according to a poll conducted last year by the *Rand Daily Mail*, a Johannesburg newspaper that recently folded. This figure does not include the police, who are heavily armed. In June 1976 protests by students in the Soweto township over Afrikaner language requirements sparked widespread uprisings. By the time all was quiet, 700 people had been killed— according to *official* records—most shot dead by police. Fearing arrest in connection with the demonstrations, Temba fled the country.

THE SUM OF TH

Taking the measure of Bush

You will not find the name Maxwell Gluck on this State Department list of Bush administration ambassadors, but he is here in spirit. Gluck, whom foreign service officers still speak of, was Eisenhower's nominee in 1957 to be ambassador to Ceylon, but he might have been a creation of Evelyn Waugh. He could not name Ceylon's prime minister. Asked to characterize U.S. relations with Ceylon, he responded: "I think they are a people who are friendly and unfriendly." Owner of a chain of women's-apparel stores, Gluck believed he had proved he could serve the President the previous fall, when he'd contributed $30,000 to his campaign. Alas, the Senate thought otherwise and sent him home. That was then; this is now: President Bush and a pliant Senate eager to appear "bipartisan" have seen to it that one "Gluck" after another has been hurriedly posted to this or that country—a corps that may be the least qualified (and most oleaginous) in recent history. To name a few:

C. Howard Wilkins. Foreign service experience: none. Contribution to Republican party, 1988: $100,000.

Frederick M. Bush. Not related to the President but, politically speaking, real family: He's been (G.) Bush's top political fund-raiser for the past ten years. Speaks neither French nor German nor Letzeburgesch but apparently has a grasp of Luxembourg's tourist-driven economy: He listed among his qualifications that he is "an avid squash and tennis player." Caribbean would seem to have been more appropriate area for posting: (F.) Bush, according to investigators into the HUD scandal, was paid a $160,000 "consulting fee" for a rehab project in Puerto Rico. Fact that he admitted never having actually visited the site may have ruled out island posting.

Donald Gregg. National Security Adviser to V.P. Bush, valued for his golden silence. Has close ties to Felix Rodriguez—the ex-CIA agent recruited by Oliver North to serve as liaison between the Salvadoran Air Force and private American crews involved in the Contra resupply effort—and in January '85 brought Bush and Rodriguez together for a meeting. Yet maintained throughout '88 campaign—and during his confirmation hearing—that Bush knew nothing of illegal (because of Boland Amendment) resupply. Previous Asian experience: CIA officer, Vietnam.

Murray Waas is an independent reporter who writes frequently on national security and foreign policy matters. His articles have appeared in The Boston Globe, the Washington Post, The Nation, *and* The Village Voice, *as well as* Harper's.

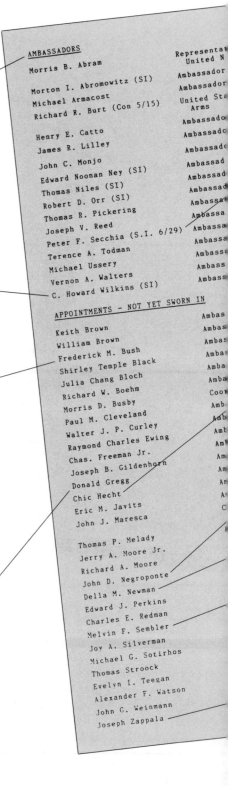

```
AMBASSADORS                          Representat
                                     United N
Morris B. Abram
                                     Ambassador
Morton I. Abromowitz (SI)            Ambassador
Michael Armacost                     United Sta
Richard R. Burt (Con 5/15)             Arms
                                     Ambassado
Henry E. Catto                       Ambassado
James R. Lilley                      Ambassado
John C. Monjo                        Ambassad
Edward Noonan Ney (SI)               Ambassad
Thomas Niles (SI)                    Ambassad
Robert D. Orr (SI)                   Ambassa
Thomas R. Pickering                  Ambassa
Joseph V. Reed                       Ambassa
Peter F. Secchia (S.I. 6/29)         Ambassa
Terence A. Todman                    Ambass
Michael Ussery                       Ambass
Vernon A. Walters                    Ambass
C. Howard Wilkins (SI)               Ambass

APPOINTMENTS - NOT YET SWORN IN
                                     Ambas
Keith Brown                          Ambas
William Brown                        Ambas
Frederick M. Bush                    Amba
Shirley Temple Black                 Amba
Julia Chang Bloch                    Amba
Richard W. Boehm                     Coo
Morris D. Busby                      Amb
Paul M. Cleveland                    Amb
Walter J. P. Curley                  Amb
Raymond Charles Ewing                Am
Chas. Freeman Jr.                    Am
Joseph B. Gildenhorn                 Am
Donald Gregg                         Am
Chic Hecht                           A
Eric M. Javits                       A
John J. Maresca                      C

Thomas P. Melady
Jerry A. Moore Jr.
Richard A. Moore
John D. Negroponte
Della M. Newman
Edward J. Perkins
Charles E. Redman
Melvin F. Sembler
Joy A. Silverman
Michael G. Sotirhos
Thomas Stroock
Evelyn I. Teegan
Alexander F. Watson
John G. Weinmann
Joseph Zappala
```

IR POSSESSIONS

nbassadors, *by Murray Waas*

e European Office of the
y
iator for Strategic Nuclear
United Kingdom
a
nesia
ada
European Community – Brussels
gapore
e UN
f of Protocol
aly
rgentina
orocco (Hold-over)
he Federal Republic of Germany
etherlands

Denmark
Israel
Luxembourg
Czechoslovakia
Nepal
Oman (Hold-over)
for Counter Terrorism
o Malaysia
o France
to Ghana
to Saudi Arabia
to Switzerland
to Korea
to the Bahamas
to Venezuela
he US Delegation to the Negotiations
idence and Security Building Measures
r to the Holy See
r to Lesotho
or to Ireland
or to Mexico
or to New Zealand
General of the Foreign Service
dor to Sweden
dor to Australia
dor to Barbados
ador to Greece
ador to Guatemala
ador to Tonga and Tuvala (Fiji)
eputy Representative to the United Nations
sador to Finland
sador to Spain

Peter F. Secchia. Lumber tycoon who engineered Bush's crucial Michigan caucus victory in January '88. Perhaps expects to find in Rome what he told a reporter for this magazine he was looking for at '87 state Republican conference: "a big-titted woman."

Chic Hecht. No friend of Bush's but a friend of Bob Dole's; appointment a fence-mending gesture. Hecht, a one-term Nevada senator, told the Senate Foreign Relations Committee: "I am sure I will feel at home in the Bahamas. I've been involved in gambling in Nevada and I've been involved in banking." Reflecting, perhaps, an understanding of job's postcolonial *cultural* dimension, he added: "I love golf and they have a lot of nice golf courses."

John D. Negroponte. Reagan ambassador to Honduras. May or may not have played a key role in Iran-Contra "quid pro quo" (the deal in which U.S. gave aid to Honduras in exchange for Honduran aid to the Contras) that Bush may or may not have played a key role in. This may or may not mean that Bush owes Negroponte. (*See* Gregg, "golden silence.")

Della M. Newman. Seattle real estate broker who chaired Bush campaign in Washington State. In interview, noted she has no particular interest in foreign affairs. Could not name New Zealand's prime minister (David Lange) when asked by a reporter to do so. Later maintained she *did* know his name but kept mum because she didn't know the correct—New Zealandish?—pronunciation.

Melvin F. Sembler. Foreign service experience: none. Contribution to Republican party, 1988: $100,000.

Joseph Zappala. His $100,000 contribution had nothing to do with it! Because there is both real estate and drug abuse in Spain, the Bush administration has been quick to point out that Zappala's work as a developer and as a cofounder (with Melvin Sembler) of Straight, Inc., a drug-rehab program, qualifies him for this post. Curiously, officials have failed to mention that inspectors for Florida's Department of Health and Rehabilitative Services found that Straight incarcerated adults and children against their will and abused them. In '83, Fred Collins, nineteen, was awarded a $220,000 judgment against Straight after a federal jury found that he had been falsely imprisoned by Straight for 130 days.

THIS TIME, IT

An anxious gloss of a l

I am one of the estimated 1,000,000 to 1,500,000 people in the United States whose blood carries antibodies for the human immunodeficiency virus (HIV). The antibodies are an ominous signal: Researchers suspect that 20 to 40 percent of us will develop, in the next seven years, acquired immune deficiency syndrome (AIDS). No one knows why some of us will contract AIDS only months after infection while others won't develop symptoms for years, perhaps never. I found out two years ago that I'm HIV-positive. Every three months I have my blood drawn and tested to monitor my condition. It takes a week for the results to come back. This period of waiting arouses great anxiety. Will the lab results tell me I'm getting sick? If I do get sick, will my friends be able to take care of me? Will I die soon? How much time do I have?

I've been forced to learn more biochemistry than I'd ever dreamed of. I now know that mature T cells, B cells, and natural killer cells are all indexes of my body's response to infection. Most of these measurements are high; my body knows something is going on and is mounting a defense. But the very low ratio of helper to suppressor cells indicates the problem. Helper cells activate the immune system; suppressor cells slow it down. By attacking the helper cells, HIV is throwing my immune system into disarray. My ratio is much lower than normal, the lowest it's ever been.

It's expensive to find out if I am getting sick. This report cost me $270, not including the office visit. I usually donate my blood to a research institute in order to avoid this expense. Many of us infected with HIV have made this kind of trade, turning ourselves into test subjects in return for experimental drugs or high-tech lab work we couldn't otherwise receive or afford. Like many other people with HIV, I don't want to alert my insurance company about my status until it's necessary or submit a claim for this test as long as I can afford not to. In every state but California, insurance companies have the legal right to deny health insurance to applicants who test positive for the virus. The longer my insurance policy is in effect, the harder it will be for the company to deny me benefits. The cost of AIDS treatment is enormous, and I fear that the insurance company will refuse to pay for my care if given any way to do so.

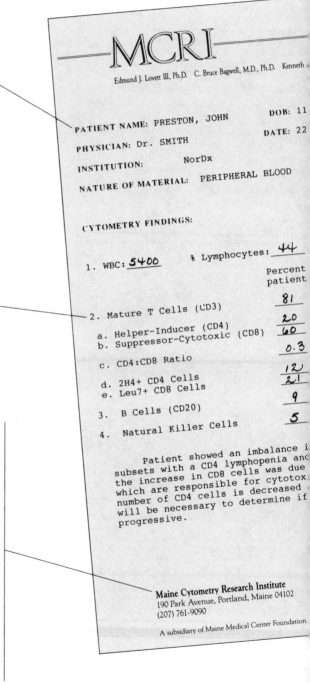

MCRI

Edmund J. Lovett III, Ph.D. C. Bruce Bagwell, M.D., Ph.D. Kenneth

PATIENT NAME: PRESTON, JOHN DOB: 11

PHYSICIAN: Dr. SMITH DATE: 22

INSTITUTION: NorDx

NATURE OF MATERIAL: PERIPHERAL BLOOD

CYTOMETRY FINDINGS:

1. WBC: 5400 % Lymphocytes: 44

	Percent patient
2. Mature T Cells (CD3)	81
a. Helper-Inducer (CD4)	20
b. Suppressor-Cytotoxic (CD8)	60
c. CD4:CD8 Ratio	0.3
d. 2H4+ CD4 Cells	12
e. Leu7+ CD8 Cells	21
3. B Cells (CD20)	9
4. Natural Killer Cells	5

Patient showed an imbalance i subsets with a CD4 lymphopenia and the increase in CD8 cells was due which are responsible for cytotox number of CD4 cells is decreased will be necessary to determine if progressive.

Maine Cytometry Research Institute
190 Park Avenue, Portland, Maine 04102
(207) 761-9090

A subsidiary of Maine Medical Center Foundation

COULD BE AIDS

report, *by John Preston*

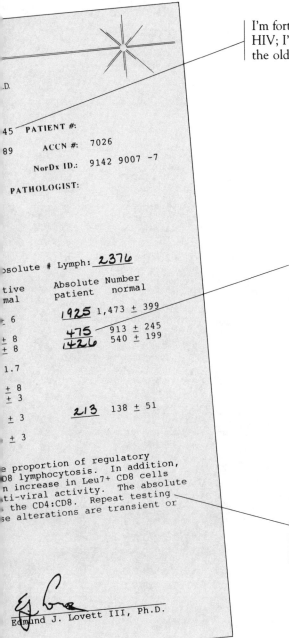

I'm forty-four. I know dozens of people infected with HIV; I've known dozens who have died of AIDS. I'm the oldest of us all.

This is the number I really want to know about. The absolute count of the helper-inducer cell—often called the T4 cell—is used to measure the actual strength of the immune system. T4 counts can be maddeningly volatile. The wide use of this test gives the impression that this is a definite measure of mortality, an impression hard to ignore when one is HIV-positive. I panicked the time my score went below 300, sure I was about to become ill; I was euphoric the one time it went over 700, hoping against all scientific belief that I might beat the infection. In fact, no one test can be trusted. What's important is the trend. My tests have generally stayed in the high 400s. That stability provides some encouragement. My count is about one half of normal, just what's expected of someone who is HIV-positive but has not shown symptoms of AIDS. It indicates that my immune system is still adequate to fight off disease. As with many other people, my system won't tolerate AZT. If the count falls below 200, I'll be eligible for experimental drugs. A count below 100 usually signals full-blown AIDS.

Repeat testing is a way of life for me. I can relax for a while now. But in three months I'll again go through my week of wondering and once again have to live with the fear that my body is going to fail me, that I may be developing AIDS.

John Preston is writer-in-residence at the AIDS Project in Portland, Maine. He is the editor of Personal Dispatches: Writers Confront AIDS *(St. Martin's) and* Hometown: Gay Men Write about Where They Belong *(Dutton). He is author of* The Big Gay Book: A Man's Survival Guide for the 90's *(NAL/Plume).*

A hoary developer's adage runs thus: To build a bad building, hire a good architect; to build an outrageous building, hire a distinguished one. This particular ensemble of outrages, the big new Forty-second Street development project, is the work of Philip Johnson—Peck's Bad Boy of the *haute bourgeoisie*, erstwhile collaborator of Mies van der Rohe on the Seagram building, lately avatar of postmodernism. The mansard roof used here four times is the absolute totem of kitsch good taste. Think of McDonald's: the original burger outlets were, like Times Square, glitzy, exuberant, awash in neon. But before long, the chain, courting the ersatz respectability of Middle America, topped its stands with the mansards that crown so many gas stations, branch banks, and other architectural effluvia on the strip. Johnson takes them Forty-second Street: the homogeneous overwhelms the genius loci.

These big squares are known in the business as scaling devices. The basic "problem" in designing big slab office buildings is devising ways to obscure their bulk—camouflage. Johnson uses three decorator tactics to this end: shifts in material; appliquéd ornaments; and shifts in proportion. The last works like this: if one assigns one of the little grid squares in the black glass background the value of "one," each small window, with four squares, will have the value of four of these; each big central window, then, with sixteen squares, will have the value of four windows. This modulation makes the tower look positively lithesome, yes? True, Johnson's system is somewhat lacking in sophistication, requiring, as it does, no more than mastery of the lower reaches of the two-times table. Then again, no such two-dimensional configuring can ever really bulk too large in reducing too-large bulk.

This red granite base is an evasion of one of the key recommendations in the design guidelines. Instead of offering a five-story "street wall" base, with the tower set back above it, Johnson presents buildings that rise straight up—thereby capturing a greater volume of leasable space for the developer. The change in materials is offered as a graphic substitute—as if that could compensate for the daylight kept from the street by the absence of setbacks.

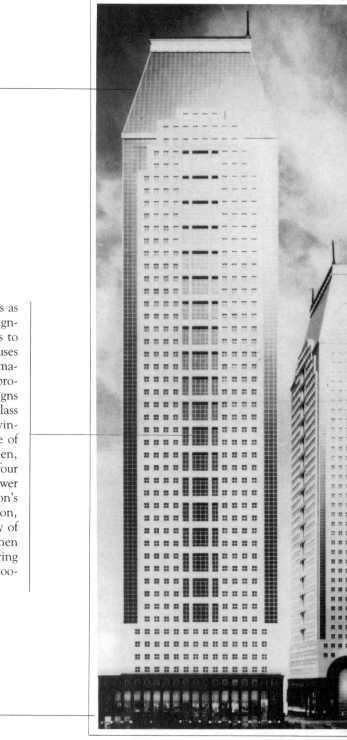

CLEANSING OF 42ND ST.

painting, *by Michael Sorkin*

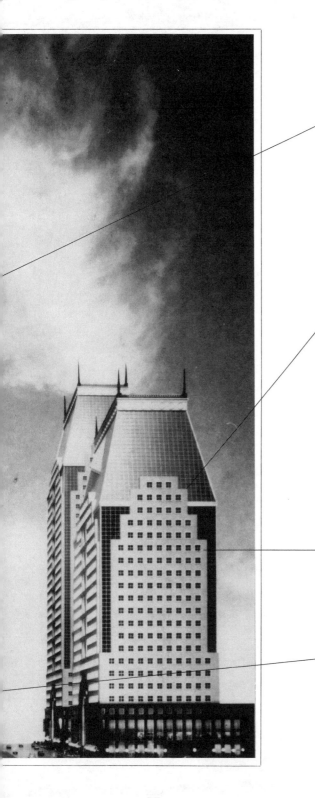

Ornament is crime—or so said the architect Adolph Loos. These pathetic rooftop gewgaws are merely misdemeanors. Aggressive bad taste has always been a potent tool of the gentrifier. Like all kitsch, this is an address from above to the teeming, threatening, consuming masses. Here, from the very top, a bit of smug Johnsonian camp: *Let them eat wedding cake!*

The stepped forms encourage one to read these limestone faces against the dark glass backgrounds as if they were, in fact, *separate buildings*. Cruel joke: Johnson "pastes" on his thuggish towers imaginary buildings of a more appropriate scale and skinniness. Yet another graphic substitute for real design activity that, instead of admitting air to the street, simply gives the air to the public.

Square is the preferred window shape of the 1980s, a vogue largely attributable to the Italian cult-architect Aldo Rossi, for whom such openings represent near ur-fenestration. The crossbars in Johnson's windows connote operability, but their real purpose is graphic. The cross does abet an additional conceit—the illusion that the stone face is actually laid over a background of dark, gridded glass. The conceit, a popular one in New York these days, has been rendered with great panache by Cesar Pelli, from whose buildings Johnson shamelessly, if ineptly, appropriates it.

Johnson's current signature is the arched entry portal, and to make sure it isn't missed, he repeats it four times—a multiple in the manner of, say, Gloria Vanderbilt. The arched entranceway here is taken, of course, from Johnson's own best-publicized icon, the AT&T building on Madison Avenue in midtown Manhattan. *That* entry was itself cribbed from the late, great Brunelleschi.

Michael Sorkin, an architect and writer, teaches at Yale University, Cooper Union College, and the Southern California Institute of Architecture.

Redevelopment as pork

A boondoggle from base to capital, the $1.6 billion Forty-second Street development project supposedly will "eliminate blight on Forty-second Street between Broadway and Eighth Avenue." Most of the thirteen-acre project area, better known as Times Square, will by 1986 have been demolished (the Times Tower included), to be replaced by four huge office towers, a 700-room hotel, and a two-block-long wholesale trade mart—all this courtesy of the New York State Urban Development Corporation. The UDC's sweeping condemnation powers made land acquisition cheaper and easier. UDC involvement also means that the two biggest buildings (the biggest is fifty-six stories) can soar twice as high as heretofore allowed in the area—which translates as twice as many rentable floors for developer George Klein. Klein also gets a fifteen-year tax abatement, which comes to at least $650 million. Incentives indeed. A prominent developer, Klein figures prominently in Ed Koch's best seller, *Mayor*. George, says Ed, is "at the top of the list of my campaign contributors."

It won't be all work, no play for the young despots in training spending their days here. High-priced lunch-time diversions will replace fast food and double features on the street. At present, "users of the street," as the planners say, are mostly black and/or poor. Some are criminals, though the UDC is careful to note that "the distinction between legitimate and illegitimate uses of the street is not easily made. . . . Those standing around . . . in front of a movie theater often appear as ominous as the pushers." Solution? Can't discriminate between, discriminate against: give them what they don't want (fern bars, boutiques) and you accomplish wholesale Negro removal.

The porno venders chased from Forty-second Street will end up here, north of Times Square, where there is already a smattering of peep shows and adult bookshops. Unlike the younger, poorer, and darker crowds drawn to Times Square for big-screen action, those after erotic thrills tend to be white, middle-class males. On the street, they look just like respectable businessmen.

D. D. Guttenplan is a former senior editor at The Village Voice *and a former media columnist for* New York Newsday. *He is currently at work on a biography of I. F. Stone.*

barrel, *by D. D. Guttenplan*

Nearly one fifth of all clothing made in the USA comes from New York's garment district, a twenty-block area just south of this tower. More than 140,000 people work there. But not for long. The half-million square feet of apparel showroom space to be available in the project's Eighth Avenue merchandise mart is an open invitation to cheap imports and out-of-town manufacturers. And the rise in demand for higher-rent office space in the area may well force low-rent manufacturing lofts out of the city. The result? According to both the ILGWU and the Federation of Apparel Manufacturers, the end of New York's largest manufacturing industry.

Just west of these towers will remain the twenty-five-story Candler building. In February 1980 the building was sold to former New York City Taxi and Limousine Commissioner Michael J. Lazar—a bargain at only $1.3 million. Just how much of a bargain became clear not long after, when, as one of the only structures in the project area not scheduled for condemnation or demolition, the Candler building suddenly became an extremely valuable piece of real estate. While the fortunate Lazar waits for the neighborhood to improve around him, he has been given a helping hand by his friends at the Taxi and Limousine Commission, which rents out four floors of what would otherwise be a mostly empty building. Another floor has been taken by the Vera Institute, a research group once headed by Herbert Sturz, who now serves as New York's planning commissioner. It may be that Lazar's political benefactions since acquiring his building—$7,500 to Governor Mario Cuomo, $7,600 to Mayor Koch, $5,000 to city Comptroller Harrison Goldin—are his way of sharing his happiness with those who (in a very real way) made it all possible.

Twenty-one thousand new jobs for Times Square—this according to project boosters. These are new jobs like the '72 Impala I bought last summer is my new car. Most of those who will come to work in these towers—like the lawyers at Dewey, Ballantine, Bushby, Palmer and Wood, the only tenants so far—will simply be changing Manhattan addresses.

Many of the new breed hanging out in Times Square will walk home from work. Clinton, better known as Hell's Kitchen, is just a few blocks away and ripe for gentrification and further speculation. But that is the point of all this, isn't it?

THE REA

A quick read on book coll

The signature belongs to Henry James, and the inscription to his friend Walter Berry is in a 1904 first edition of James's *The Golden Bowl*. This splendid "presentation copy" (a gift from the author) rated a full page in the Christie's catalogue issued last January for the auction of the estate of James Gilvarry, a book lover who died in 1984. First editions—plain, signed, or inscribed—trade in a market as efficient as that on Wall Street. Gilvarry, a Bernard Baruch among book collectors, began to buy first editions of James in the 1930s, when they were selling for ten or fifteen dollars. His collection sat in a small, dark apartment in Manhattan, appreciating like a portfolio of IBM.

The Golden Bowl was lot 103 in the Christie's sale, which attracted all the major book dealers, some representing the handful of wealthy collectors who dominate the market. (For the price of a very minor Monet, which is to say a million dollars, an individual can become a very major book collector.) Collectors generally stay away from the big auctions; if they tried to bid for themselves, the dealers would make sure that they got no bargains. What Isaac Babel wrote of librarians in Odessa is true of book dealers: "they have entered into communion with The Book, with life at second-hand." The atmosphere in the auction room when books are on the block is accordingly mustier than, say, when there is a sale of Postimpressionist paintings.

When Gilvarry started to buy James, dealers were delighted to include for free postcards and letters he had signed (now, like the card signed by James and Edith Wharton noted here, worth thousands). At the time, James's reputation was being sat on by Marxist critics, who later changed their minds about an author who could write of "the black and merciless things that are behind great possessions." As late as the early 1960s, lot 103 might have been acquired for a few hundred dollars.

● 103 JAMES, HENRY. The Golden Bowl,
original tannish-rose sateen cloth, t.e.g., other e
EDITION, PRESENTATION COPY TO WALTER BERRY,
James, November 1904" (publication month).
Edith Wharton and James to Berry in Washingt
tour in France in March 1907, addressed by Wha
"Les Sandistes saluent, en route pour Nohant. M
BAL 10659; Edel & Laurence A60a. The Harry
volume. Walter Van Rensselaer Berry (1859-1
Parisian social and literary circles, was an early a
good friend of James. The letters from James to
Sun Press in 1928 (see lot 116). When Berry die
Harry Crosby (of The Black Sun Press). In a lett
ed. Edel, IV, p. 334), James writes: ". . . I am
Bowl which comes out tomorrow. The Scribne
comparatively brazen about thrusting it on peo
this sense I would in fact send a copy to [Walte
very kindly inscribe the same on a simple card a

George Sim Johnston, a serendipitous book collector, is a writer living in New York City. He has just completed a novel on Wall Street in the eighties.

THINGS

g, by George Sim Johnston

The most important item in a catalogue is the description of a book's condition. The ideal copy is one that has never been opened, unless the original owner was famous and given to scribbling in the margins. Twentieth-century authors must come dressed in dust jacket.. A first edition of *The Great Gatsby* in a mint jacket might go to a collector for $5,000. Without the jacket, the same copy of *Gatsby* might be worth only $100.

The critic Philip Rahv once made a distinction between writers who are "palefaces" and those who are "redskins." Collectors, like academics, prefer the former. Mandarins like Joyce (presentation copy of a first edition of *Ulysses*, $38,500) and T. S. Eliot (first edition of *Prufrock*, $2,200) generally fetch much higher prices than Mark Twain or Theodore Dreiser. This Christie's blurb is a veritable précis of paleface culture. James was the prince of palefaces, and Berry, who may or may not have been Edith Wharton's lover, was a Washington lawyer who was most at home in a Parisian drawing room. Harry Crosby, the owner of the bookplates, took paleface culture the full circle by performing strange onanistic rites while chanting hymns to the sun.

rk: Charles Scribner's Sons 1904, *2 vols., 8vo,*
t, portions faded, a little soiled, slipcase, FIRST
by the author: "To Walter V.R. Berry, Henry
s an Autograph picture postcard signed from
vhile the Whartons and James were on a motor
with a note by her on the picture (of a church):
. E.W.''; this is followed by James's signature.
esse Crosby copy, with their bookplate in each
ealthy bibliophile and a well-known figure in
ed friend of Edith Wharton who also became a
ere published in a limited edition by The Black
ueathed virtually all of his library to his cousin
th Wharton dated November 18, 1904 (*Letters,*
g to send you an advance-copy of *The Golden*
ade so pretty a pair of volumes of it that I am
type and paper are so pleasing! Sustained by
n Washington if I had his address. Would you
o me?" (2)

$2,000-3,000

The book market has fads and panics just like the stock market. In the late 1970s, the book market was overbought by investors who were dumping stocks and swapping into "tangibles"; a selling wave subsequently gripped New York and London, driving the prices of many authors down. The Christie's sale, however, confirmed the long-term bull market for Henry James. And lot 103—in Jamesian locution—produced some of the finer vibrations in the auction room that day. It was conservatively estimated to go for $2,000–$3,000; it went for $17,600.

THE CURREN

An account of Swiss ba

Like you, I knew about Swiss banks, or thought I did. I'd seen the James Bond movies; I'd heard that Sanjay Gandhi had the number of his account engraved on the back of his watch. I knew Swiss banks were safe and stable. And I knew Swiss bankers could keep a secret. So I walked into the Davos branch of the Swiss Bank Corporation last summer and told the teller I had come—like Marcos and "Baby Doc"—to open a *numbered account*. The Davos branch already had nearly 2,000 of these accounts, most of them opened by Germans or Americans. I was going to add my $100 to the $1 trillion foreigners have on deposit in Swiss banks.

Although they profit from it, Swiss bankers don't like their image as accessories to crime. The "Agreement on the Observance of Care by the Banks in Accepting Funds and on the Practice of Banking Secrecy" adopted by the Swiss Bankers' Association requires that banks ascertain the identity of their customers "on a systematic basis," and it prohibits bankers from opening accounts for the purpose of capital flight or tax evasion. According to the association, Swiss banks may open numbered accounts only "when the bank has established through interviews . . . that [a customer] has legitimate reasons for wishing this protection." At the SBC branch in Davos, they interviewed my passport. But at another of the country's major banks, Crédit Suisse, where I also inquired about opening an account, I was asked why I wished to do so. "I am told this is the thing to do," I replied. My banker seemed reassured.

Documentation, or lack thereof, is a key to secrecy. In earlier days—such as after the French Revolution, when Swiss bankers served an aristocracy under siege—bank statements and the like were carried outside the country before being mailed in order not to compromise the clients. Today, for a small fee, Swiss banks will retain the evidence of all account transactions.

Y OF SECRECY

g, by Robert Karl Manoff

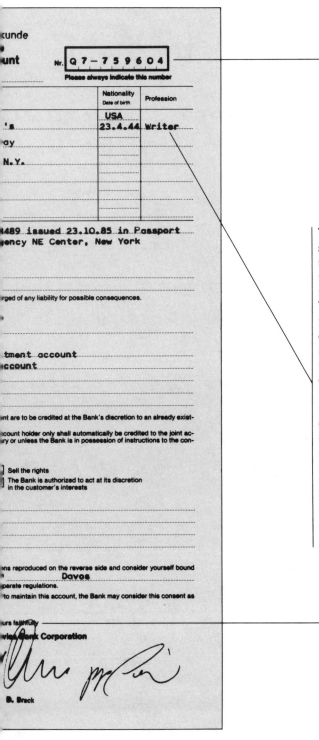

This is my number. It was assigned to me by the bank and must be included in all correspondence along with my signature, of which the bank kept a sample. My account is identified only by number in all bank records. Only the branch manager, his assistant, and several other officers have access to the vault where this document and a few others I signed associate my name with the account. Swiss law makes it a crime punishable by up to six months in prison and a 50,000 franc ($31,000) fine for a bank employee to divulge information about any bank transaction.

The man at Crédit Suisse was relieved I wasn't a stockbroker. Insider trading has made brokers unpopular with the bankers, since American investigations of such activity have resulted in major breaches of banking secrecy. The 1977 Treaty on Mutual Assistance in Criminal Matters requires Swiss banks to open up their records for American investigations of crimes that are also crimes in Switzerland; but in recent years the U.S. government has brought pressure on the Swiss to cooperate with investigations of insider trading, even though such trading is not a violation of Swiss law. Under Agreement XVI of the Swiss Bankers' Association, all American clients must sign a form stating that if their accounts have been used to trade on U.S. markets, their bank records may be made available to U.S. investigators. Under the agreement, banks may also seize Americans' accounts if the SEC suspects they contain funds derived from insider trading—bad news for those who have plans to emulate Dennis Levine.

Now for the good news: tax evasion is still not a crime in Switzerland. And neither Swiss banks nor the Swiss government will assist an American investigation of unreported income. That is the bottom line.

Robert Karl Manoff is a contributing editor of Harper's Magazine.

Deceased is a legal word, one which, most grammarians agree, is pretentious in any other context. Its virtue as a legal term lies in the very qualities that otherwise make it coy. It is distancing, death in a business suit. Not as saccharine as *departed*; not as raw as *corpse*. And it has a chronological nuance: it means not just dead, but recently dead.

Use of a room in the funeral home for a three-hour "visitation" costs about $370; that's a little over $2 a minute, about what a good psychoanalyst gets. *Visitation* hints at haunting, but it is the living who are visiting the dead, the mourners who haunt the corpse.

A crucifix, cross, or Star of David costs $16—the cheapest items on a funeral home's price list. This is one of the few places in the contract where religion is mentioned. At least contractually, a funeral home is no more concerned with spiritual values than a store that rents tuxedos for prom night is concerned with love.

Clothing or burial garments cost from $20 to $600. We would no more wrap a corpse in a shroud than wear a sheet to a restaurant. We dress our dead as if they were alive. Many are given clothes to wear after death that are more expensive and fancier than anything they may have worn while alive—as if death were a job promotion.

The charge for the hearse ranges from $176 to $239—plus tolls. Although the funeral procession rides along real roads in the real world, this charge brings to mind various myths in which the spirits of the dead pay fees to pass through some mortal checkpoint: the hearse as a cosmic taxi, replacing the ferry across the river Lethe.

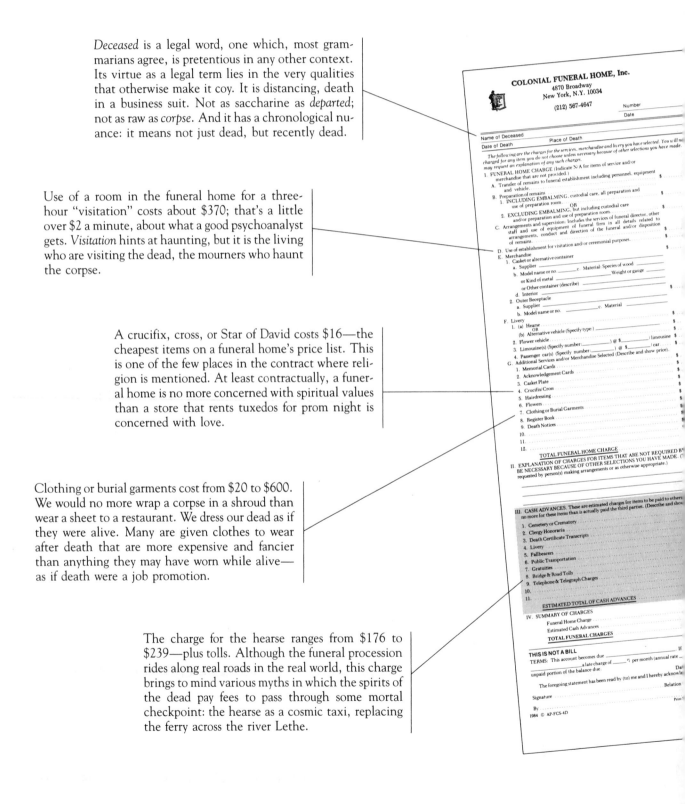

ABOUT THE DEAD

meanings, *by David Black*

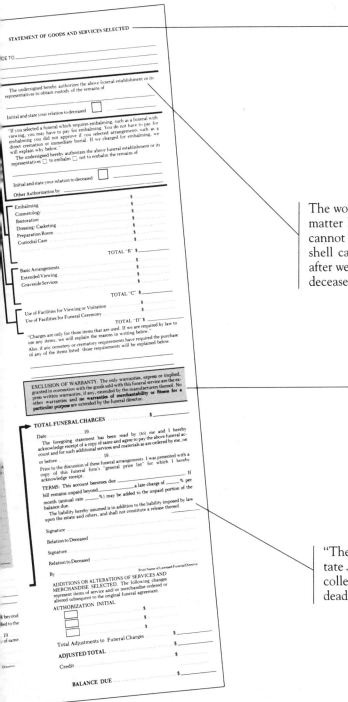

These commercial terms—*goods* and *services*—reflect the notion that the dead are consumers. But, like newborns, their needs tend to be overshadowed by the needs of those who must take care of them. The expensive casket (at prices as high as $7,700), like the expensive bassinet, is not intended for the comfort of the body using it. A corpse needs nothing—not casket, not flowers (which range from $25 to $1,500), not even grief. If the soul exists, it certainly has no elaborate material needs. The goods and services reassure the living of their social standing, of their place in this world.

The word *remains* suggests garbage. The living, no matter how solemn and sincere our grief may be, cannot help but see the body as either the rotting shell cast off by the soul or those parts left over after we have emotionally feasted on the life of the deceased.

This refusal to grant a warranty for "fitness for a particular purpose" undoubtedly protects the funeral home when a grieving widow freaks out on realizing that she has chosen to bury a loved one in an object that under other circumstances she would find gaudy or crass. At funerals, people who otherwise show no indication of being tacky or lacking in common sense abandon good taste in the effort to maintain it.

"The liability... imposed by law upon the estate..." If the bereaved welsh on the deal, the bill collector will knock on the tomb door. You can be dead, it would seem, but not a deadbeat.

David Black is the author of Minds *and* Murder at the Met, *among other books, and the producer of the television series* Law and Order.

ARAFAT'S TYPE

A close reading of a historic P

The theories of literary critic William Empson aren't big on campus anymore, but they seem to have made a comeback among Mideast experts: when Yasir Arafat read the Palestinian Declaration of Independence last November, commentators seldom failed to mention Empson's beloved "ambiguity." But, whereas New Critic Empson reveled in ambiguity, the old critics of the Palestinians used the word either to dismiss the declaration or as an excuse to not really read it at all. The *New York Times*'s editorial on the text and the other Palestine National Council resolutions ran under the headline LESS THAN MEETS THE EYE. What New Critic would have ever believed that! Herewith, a close reading of this historic text.

In the opening paragraph, as elsewhere, one hears echoes of the 1948 Israeli Declaration of Independence. In the Palestinian text, Palestine "is where the Palestinian Arab people was born, on which it grew, developed and excelled"; the Israeli declaration states: "Eretz Israel was the birthplace of the Jewish people. Here their spiritual, religious and political identity was shaped." Both the Palestinian and Israeli warmer-uppers would seem to assert a natural historic right to all the land from Jordan to the sea. The Palestinians, however, as the rest of the text shows, recognize that, inevitably, they have to trade down the broad homeland of the mind for a narrow state underfoot.

This is, perhaps, the most important statement in the declaration: the acceptance in writing of the principle of partition. It rescinds the notorious Article 19 of the Palestinian National Charter, which states: "The partition of Palestine in 1947 and the establishment of the state of Israel are entirely illegal." This means that the Palestine National Council accepts a two-state solution (reinforced by acceptance below of all UN resolutions, including, necessarily, 273, which admitted Israel to the UN in 1949). Is it ambiguous? *Of course.* It is a basis for negotiation. It is *not*, as Israeli officials would have it, a clear implication that the PNC wants the two states to return to the proposed 1947 borders, borders beyond which Israel has unambiguously expanded. The fact is, Israel *has* no fixed borders today. And nobody, but nobody, in Israel's current coalition government talks about a two-state solution. No ambiguity there.

Anton Shammas, an Israeli-Palestinian, is the author of Arabesques, *a novel.*

OPINION

Declaration Of

In last week's Al-Fajr we published an unofficial translation of the Palestinian Declaration of Independence. Following is the official translation by Professor Edward Said.

In the name of God,
the Compassionate,
the Merciful

Palestine, the Land of the three monotheistic faiths, is where the Palestinian Arab people was born, on which it grew, developed and excelled. The Palestinian people was never separated from or diminished in its integral bonds with Palestine. Thus the Palestinian Arab people ensured for itself an everlasting union between itself, its land and its history.

Resolute throughout that history, the Palestinian Arab people forged its national identity, rising even to unimagined levels in its defense, as invasion, the design of others, and the appeal special to Palestine's ancient and luminous place on that eminence where powers and civilizations are joined.... All this intervened thereby to deprive the people of its political independence. Yet the undying connection between Palestine and its people secured for the land its character, and for the people its national genius.

Nourished by an unfolding series of civilizations and cultures, inspired by a heritage rich in variety and kind, the Palestinian Arab people added to its stature by consolidating a union between itself and its patrimonial land. The call went out from Temple, Church and Mosque that to praise the Creator, to celebrate compassion and peace was indeed the message of Palestine. And in generation after generation, the Palestinian Arab people gave of itself unsparingly in the valiant battle for liberation. Our people's rebellions are the heroic embodiment of our will for national independence. And so the people was sustained in the struggle to stay and to prevail.

When in the course of modern times a new order of values was declared with norms and values fair for all, it was the Palestinian Arab people that had been excluded from the destiny of all other peoples by a hostile array of local and foreign powers. Yet again had unaided justice been revealed as insufficient to drive the world's history along its preferred course.

And it was the Palestinian people, already wounded in its body, that was submitted to yet another type of occupation over which floated the falsehood that "Palestine was a land without people." This notion was foisted upon some in the world, whereas in Article 22 of the Covenant of the League of Nations (1919) and in the Treaty of Lausanne (1923), the community of nations had recognized that all the Arab territories, including Palestine of the formerly Ottoman provinces, were to have granted to them their freedom as provisionally independent nations.

Despite the historical injustice inflicted on the Palestinian Arab people resulting in their dispersion and depriving them of their right to self-determination, following upon UN General Assembly Resolution 181 (1947), which partitioned Palestine into

two states, one Arab, one Jewish, it is this resolution that still provides the conditions for international legitimacy that guarantees the right of the Palestinian Arab people to sovereignty on their homeland.

By stages, the occupation of Palestine and parts of other Arab territories by Israeli forces, the willed dispossession and expulsion from their ancestral homes of the majority of Palestine's civilian inhabitants was achieved by organized terror; those Palestinians who remained, as a vestige subjugated in its homeland, were persecuted and forced to endure the destruction of their national life.

Thus were principles of international legitimacy violated. Thus were the Charter of the United Nations and its Resolutions disfigured, for they had recognized the Palestinian Arab people's national rights, including the right of return, the right to independence, the right to sovereignty over territory and homeland.

In Palestine and on its perimeters, in exile distant and near, the Palestinian Arab people never faltered and never abandoned its conviction in its rights of return and independence. Occupation, massacres and dispersion achieved no gain in the unabated Palestinian consciousness of self and political identity, as Palestinians went forward with their destiny, undeterred and unbowed. And from out of the long years of trial in ever mounting struggle, the Palestinian political identity emerged further consolidated and confirmed. And the collective Palestinian national will forged for itself a political embodiment, the Palestine Liberation Organization, its sole legitimate representative, recognized by the world community as a whole, as well as by related regional and international institutions. Standing on the very land of conviction in the Palestinian people, of inalienable rights, and on the ground of Arab national consensus, and of international legitimacy, the PLO led the campaigns of its great people, molded into unity and powerful resolve, one and indivisible in its triumphs as it suffered massacres and confinement within and without its home. And Palestinian resistance was clarified and raised into the forefront of Arab and world awareness, as the struggle of the Palestinian Arab people achieved unique prominence among the world's liberation movements in the modern era.

The massive national uprising, the *Intifada*, now intensifying in cumulative scope and power on occupied Palestinian territories, as well as the unflinching resistance of the refugee camps outside the homeland, have elevated consciousness of the Palestinian truth and right into still higher realms of comprehension and actuality. Now at last the curtain has been dropped around a whole epoch of prevarication and negation. The *Intifada* has set siege to the mind of official Israel, which has for too long relied exclusively upon myth and terror to deny Palestinian existence altogether. Because of the *Intifada* and its revolutionary irreversible impulse, the history of Palestine has therefore arrived at a decisive juncture.

Whereas the Palestinian people reaffirms most definitively

OF AMBIGUITY
...inian text, by Anton Shammas

...land of its patrimony:
...ue of natural, and the
...rights, historical and
...ne sacrifices of succes-
...who gave of them-
...c of the freedom and
...of their homeland;
...uance of resolutions
...ab Summit Conference
...al legitimacy as em-
...the authority bestowed
...nization since 1947;
...exercise by the Palestinian
...of its rights to self-
..., political independence,
...nty over its territory;
...alestine National Council,
...of God, and in the name
...tinian Arab people; hereby
...the establishment of the
...alestine on our Palestinian
...vith its capital Jerusalem
...sh-Sharif).
...State of Palestine is the
...Palestinians wherever they
...he state is for them to enjoy
...collective national and cul-
...ntity, theirs to pursue in it a
...equality of rights. In it will
...arded their political and reli-
...onvictions and their human
...by means of a parliamentary
...atic system of governance, itself
...on freedom of expression and
...edom to form parties. The
...of minorities will duly be re-
...by the majority, as minorities
...bide by decisions of the majority.
...nance will be based on principles
...ial justice, equality and non-
...mination in public rights, men or
...n on grounds of race, religion,
...or sex under the aegis of a
...tution which ensures the rule of
...and an independent judiciary. Thus
...these principles allow no depar-
...from Palestine's age-old spiritual
...civilizational heritage of tolerance
...religious coexistence.
...The State of Palestine is an Arab
...c, an integral and indivisible part
...the Arab nation, at one with that
...ion in heritage and civilization, with
...also in its aspiration for liberation,
...ogress, democracy and unity. The
...ate of Palestine confirms its obligation
...abide by the Charter of the League
...Arab States, whereby the coordina-
...on of the Arab states with each other
...all be strengthened, it calls upon
...Arab compatriots to consolidate and
...enhance the emergence in reality of
...our state, to mobilize potential, and to
...intensify efforts whose goal is to end
...Israeli occupation.
...The State of Palestine proclaims
...its commitment to the principles and
...purposes of the United Nations, and
...to the Universal Declaration of Human
...Rights. It proclaims its commitment as
...well to the principles and policies of
...the Non-Aligned Movement.
...It further announces itself to be
...a peace-loving State, in adherence to
...the principles of peaceful coexistence.
...It will join with all states and peoples
...in order to assure a permanent peace
...based upon justice and the respect of
...rights so that humanity's potential for
...well-being may be assured, an earnest
...competition for excellence be main-
...tained, and in which confidence in the
...future will eliminate fear for those
...who are just and for whom justice is
...the only recourse.

In the context of its struggle for
peace in the Land of Love and Peace,
the State of Palestine calls upon the
United Nations to bear special responsibility for the Palestinian Arab people
and its homeland. It calls upon all
peace- and freedom-loving peoples
and states to assist it in the attainment
of its objectives, to provide it with
security, to alleviate the tragedy of its
people, and to help it terminate Israel's
occupation of the Palestinian territories.
The State of Palestine herewith
declares that it believes in the settlement of regional and international
disputes by peaceful means, in accordance with the UN Charter and resolutions. Without prejudice to its natural
right to define its territorial integrity
and independence, it therefore rejects
the threat or use of force, violence and
terrorism against its territorial integrity
or political independence, as it also
rejects their use against the territorial
integrity of other states.
Therefore, on this day unlike all
others, November 15, 1988, as we
stand at the threshold of a new dawn,
in all honor and modesty we humbly
bow to the sacred spirits of our fallen
ones, Palestinian and Arab, by the
purity of whose sacrifice for the homeland our sky has been illuminated and
our land given life. Our hearts are
lifted up and irradiated by the light
emanating from the much blessed
Intifada, from those who have endured
and have fought 'the fight of the
camps, of dispersion, of exile, from
those who have borne the standard of
freedom, our children, our aged, our
youth, our prisoners, detainees and
wounded, all those whose ties to our
sacred soil are confirmed in camp,
village and town. We render special
tribute to that brave Palestinian woman, guardian of sustenance and life,
keeper of our people's perennial flame.
To the souls of our sainted martyrs, to
the whole of our Palestinian Arab
people, to all free and honorable
peoples everywhere, we pledge that
our struggle shall be continued until
the occupation ends, and the foundation of our sovereignty and independence shall be fortified accordingly.
Therefore, we call upon our great
people to rally to the banner of Palestine, to cherish and defend it, so that it
may forever be the symbol of our
freedom and dignity in that homeland,
which is a homeland for the free, now
and always.
In the name of God, the Compassionate, the Merciful.
"Say: 'O God, Master of the
Kingdom, Thou givest the
Kingdom to whom Thou
wilt, and seizest the Kingdom from whom Thou wilt,
Thou exaltest whom Thou
wilt, and Thou abasest
whom Thou wilt; in Thy
hand is the good; Thou art
powerful over everything."
Sadaqa Allahu al-Azim

November 28, 1988, AL-FAJR, Page 5

"Dispossession," and (below) "prevarication and negation," gives it away—Edward Said wrote the official
English translation. The Arabic original is believed to
have been drafted by committee, then rewritten by
the poet Mahmoud Darwish (he is rumored to have
kept Ben-Gurion's Israeli declaration in front of him
for guidance); the Darwish text (according to Said)
was then "covered with often ludicrously clumsy in-
sertions and inexplicable deletions." Said did quite a
good job not only with the English (he is a literary
critic!) but with cutting the schmaltz in both the Arabic and the unofficial English texts. The Arabic text is
too much to chew: too large a pita, too little butter.
With declarations, as with so much else since '47, the
Jews got a better deal.

"Rejects," more than any other word, has stirred the
embers of ambiguity. Only when Arafat later tried
"renounces" did he manage to clear things up for the
State Department—though not for the Israelis, of
course. This paragraph, I should mention, draws
heavily on UN Resolution 181 (1947), which called
for each of the states to be created by partition "to
refrain in its international relations from the *threat or
use of force* [my emphases] against the territorial integrity or political independence of any State." Worth
noting, too: The Israeli Declaration of Independence
says nothing about rejecting, condemning, or re-
nouncing the use of violence—although I am sure
that there are many villagers in the Occupied Territories who wish that it did.

An unequivocally nonsecular ending—is this it for
the long-promised secular democratic state? Let's hope
it is meant only to assuage ardent Muslim groups in
Gaza and religious members of the PNC. And herein
lies my point: The Palestinian Declaration of Independence is a *political* document, a result of give-
and-take (between Palestinians), meant to inspire
give-and-take (with Israel and the other key player,
the United States). Ambiguity is the hallmark of all
such documents—I seem to remember Camp David
being *praised* for subtle ambiguities that could lead to
progress. Let me clearly state that ambiguity should be
the privilege not only of states but of stateless exiles
and refugees.

The glittering second act of Balanchine's beloved *Nutcracker*: the audience is transported from a cozy Biedermeier parlor to the Land of the Sweets. In the ballet's closing minutes the Sugar Plum Fairy and her Cavalier dance a stately and flowing grand pas de deux; just now, only seconds from the ballet's end, the Sugar Plum Fairy lowers her arms, turns to face front, and pliés. We can "read" all this in these shaded shapes and scratches, these "dance notations." Labanotation, the language written here, is not the oldest dance notation system; there have been attempts to write dance since the fifteenth century. But since it was developed by Rudolf von Laban in the 1920s, it has been the most widely used. Used to what end, though? Can any language reduce movement to marks? How do you pin down the dance?

Balanchine chose to have the ballerina be still at this point in the ballet (the open **O**). But that's Balanchine's version, for the New York City Ballet. Each year more than 200 versions of *The Nutcracker* are performed in this country, and no two are the same. E. T. A. Hoffmann wrote the tale, Tchaikovsky wrote the musical score, but Marius Petipa and Lev Ivanov did not write down their original choreography in 1892—it has been passed down like a legend, reinvented with each "telling."

This point marks the start of the Sugar Plum Fairy's two "measures" shown here. One of Laban's innovations was the three-line vertical "staff," charting the flow of dance movements from bottom to top. All the symbols appearing at the same point across a staff represent movements a dancer must make simultaneously. To read any given moment, start from the center line of the staff (representing the vertical center, or axis, of the body); the instructions to the left of this line apply to the left side of the body, and likewise for the right. Each body part—right and left foot, leg, hand, arm, etc.—has its place on the staff. The shapes and shadings of the symbols tell us in what position these body parts should be—at what height, or what angle. Here, for instance, the ballerina is (among other things) to step onto point with her right foot. The little hook attached to the hatched area that represents her right foot tells her so.

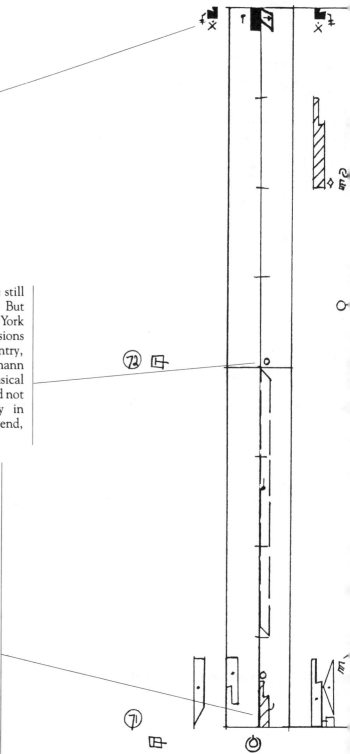

GAR PLUM FAIRY

text, *by Lois Draegin*

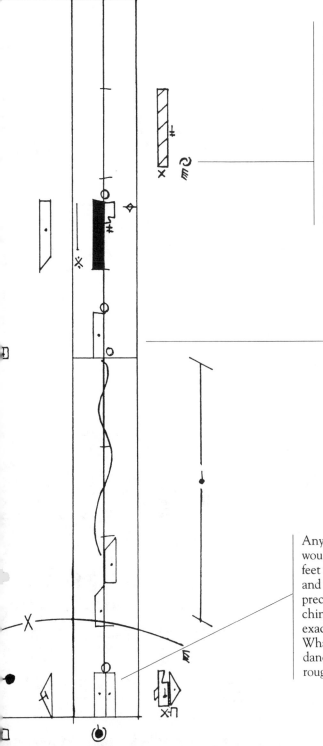

This vertical staff is for the Cavalier, and this little symbol tells him to "let go"—in this case, to let go of the hand of the Sugar Plum Fairy (whose staff we just read). Labanotation is ever being refined for elegance and concision. When notators need symbols for new movements, they draw what comes logically to mind—think of the cave painters. (To become an official part of the Labanotation language, a new symbol must be approved by an international board.) The logic of the "let go" sign is perfect: A complete, unshaded circle tells a dancer to hold his or her body just as it is. The sign to let go, to release? A circle split.

Here is our Cavalier—all he is doing is taking a step forward on his left foot. For him and for the Sugar Plum Fairy the measure is simple, and is much simpler than most measures of ballets. At this moment in *The Nutcracker*, there are only two dancers on stage, and their movements are straightforward: the Cavalier and the Sugar Plum Fairy are promenading around the stage for the most part. Scores can get complicated when, say, an entire corps of dancers is on stage. A Balanchine ballet might run 200 to 300 pages, with as many as eight staffs (as opposed to the two shown here) on a page.

Any man dancing the role of the Cavalier would, at this point in the score, stand with his feet together, his right arm extended forward—and would still look like no other dancer doing precisely the same thing. Dancers are not machines. And a dance text, for all its evolving exactness, will forever remain an open book. What is written here is choreography, not dance. Any dance notation score can be only a rough guide.

Lois Draegin is a news editor in the Arts and Entertainment department at Newsday. *She edits the Sunday "Arts and Leisure" section and directs coverage of movies, theater, and dance.*

This cluster of symbols translates as a classical "fish dive," a lift in which the female dancer is held across her partner's body—*her* body tilted toward the floor, head down, arms and legs flung behind her. The fish dive signals a climactic, romantic moment in a classical pas de deux. We can tell from the darkened symbols to the left of the staff that the Sugar Plum Fairy's left side is lowered, and we know where the Cavalier's hands should be placed to hold her. But what about the subtler movements, the "adjectives" that modify these "words"? Balanchine left these to his principals—there are some things that choreographers leave to dancers.

When Balanchine was trained, and earlier, when *The Nutcracker* was first staged, a penché arabesque—leg and arm extended back, body tilted forward—looked different than it does now. Legs were raised to hip level and tilts were shallow in the nineteenth century. When a Balanchine-trained ballerina extends her leg back, it slashes straight up, and when she tilts, she *plunges*. Would Balanchine have felt the same freedom to interpret and create—or, to put it another way, the same license to distort—if a "score" had been made of the original? Would dance have developed differently in the shadow of canonical "texts"?

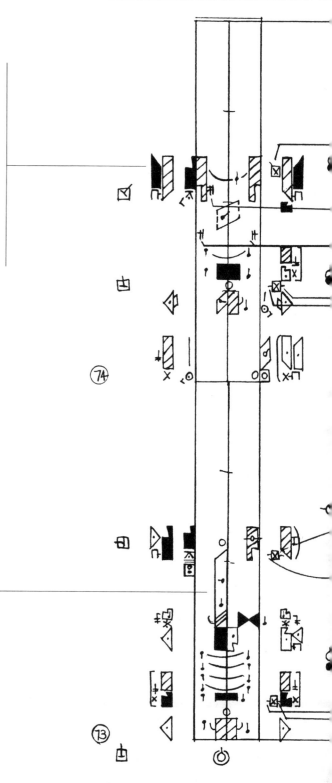

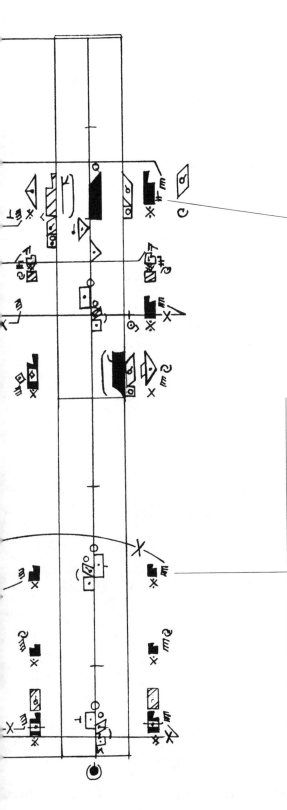

The "fish dive" in the grand pas de deux of Balanchine's Nutcracker. New York City Ballet. Sugar Plum Fairy: Patricia McBride. Cavalier: Helgi Tomasson.

For generations, Cavaliers have been stepping to the side and taking hold of their partners by the waist. We have managed to preserve this moment, this fragment of space and time, through memory and training. What would notation accomplish that this "oral" tradition has not? It is worth emphasizing that, unlike composers, choreographers do not write out their scores; notations are done by notators—by those who see the dance, not those who make it. It may well be true that dance needs its texts—what else can raise dance up from the cellar of the arts world? Art forms gain status when they develop concrete canons. But must the canon be a printed one? If musical notation had not come into existence by the 1920s, it might never have: recordings would have been the sole medium for preserving music. Already, dance is accumulating an archive of photographs, films, and videotapes—a high-tech canon. Film and video are not the perfect answers: they flatten space, and are thus poor guides to stage blocking. Maybe the Sugar Plum Fairy can deliver something IBM-compatible.

On Tuesday, April 10, 2,700 voters in the Pennsylvania presidential primary filled out this questionnaire right after casting their ballots. It is an exit poll, designed and distributed by the American Broadcasting Companies. This election year, ABC will pay ten full-time staff members and a total of 2,500 "poll takers" to gather and decipher the information volunteered by voters who fill out its questionnaire. The first exit poll, primitive by today's standards, was tested in 1967 in three obscure elections, the lieutenant governor's race in Kentucky being one of them. The brainchild of Warren Mitofsky, the director of CBS's polling operations, the first poll had a few methodological kinks. But they were ironed out by 1972, when CBS undertook a national exit poll of those who had voted in the Nixon–McGovern presidential contest. By 1980, all three networks, the Associated Press, the *New York Times*, and the *Los Angeles Times* were camping out at the voting booths.

More than 86 million Americans voted for a presidential candidate in 1980, and 36,000 of them filled out exit polls. Getting someone to fill out an exit poll—and to fill it out correctly—is not always easy. According to Mark Levy, a professor of journalism at the University of Maryland, about one out of every five voters asked to complete a questionnaire declines. There are other problems as well. Up to 10 percent of the respondents in CBS exit polls fail to fill out the second page of the questionnaire, Levy says. Also, exit polls have twice the margin of error of telephone surveys, and women, blacks, and older voters are less willing to participate in exit polls than in phone polls.

The ABC ballot does not ask voters to describe what they like most about exit polls. Let's do our own analysis. TV viewers have ever-shorter attention spans. Seeing which network makes the quickest, most accurate calls—or "characterizations" of trends, as the networks say—adds another contest to election night, making a sport of even dull, lopsided races. Let's face it: exit polls make great TV.

Eric Nadler is a writer and television producer in New York City.

PENNSYLVANIA

ABC NEWS POLL

THIS QUESTIONNAIRE IS FOR VOTERS ONLY. PLE

(IF YOU VOTED IN THE **REPUBLICAN PRIMARY** FILL OUT QUESTION 1 IN THIS COLUMN AND THEN GO TO QUESTION 2 BELOW.)

1. Did you vote in the Republican primary today? (PUT A CHECKMARK IN THE BOX NEXT TO YOUR CHOICE.)
Yes. . . . . ☐ A(
No . . . . ☐

THE REST OF THE QUESTIONS APPLY TO VOTERS
2. If the 1984 presidential election were being held today and the candidates were Ronald Reagan and Walter Mondale, for whom would you vote?
Ronald Reagan. . . . . ☐ C(
Walter Mondale . . . . ☐ (
Neither. . . . . ☐ (

3. And if the candidates were Reagan and Gar Hart, for whom would you vote?
Ronald Reagan. . . . . ☐ D(
Gary Hart. . . . . ☐ (
Neither. . . . . ☐ (

4. Which **ONE** of the personal characteristics below **BEST DESCRIBES** what you like most about Gary Hart?
He cares about people's problems . . ☐ E(
He's a strong leader . . . . ☐ (
He's experienced in government . . . ☐ (
He's independent of special interests ☐ (
He'd bring the changes the country needs . . . . ☐ (
He's clear about what he stands for. ☐ (
He's honest. . . . . ☐ (
He's concerned mainly with the issues and not his own image . . . . . ☐ (

5. Which **ONE** of the personal characteristics below **BEST DESCRIBES** what you like most about Walter Mondale?
He cares about people's problems . . ☐ F(
He's a strong leader . . . . ☐ (2
He's experienced in government . . . ☐ (3
He's independent of special interests ☐ (4
He'd bring the changes the country needs . . . . ☐ (
He's clear about what he stands for. ☐ (6
He's honest. . . . . ☐ (
He's concerned mainly with the issues and not his own image . . . . . ☐ (

EARLY RETURNS

poll, by Eric Nadler

TIME:
Before Noon ☐ (1)
Noon – 4 PM ☐ (2)
After 4 PM ☐ (3)

SECRET BALLOT

[FIL]L OUT BOTH SIDES. DO NOT SIGN YOUR NAME.

[I]F YOU VOTED IN THE **DEMOCRATIC PRIMARY** FILL
[OU]T QUESTION 1 IN THIS COLUMN AND THEN GO TO
[QU]ESTION 2 BELOW.)
[.] For whom did you vote for President? (PUT
[A] CHECKMARK IN THE BOX NEXT TO YOUR CHOICE.)

[Ga]ry Hart . . . . ☐ B(1)
[Jes]se Jackson . . . . ☐ (2)
[Wa]lter Mondale . . . . ☐ (3)
[O]ther . . . . ☐ (4)

[WI]TH THE REPUBLICAN AND DEMOCRATIC PRIMARIES
[.] Which **ONE** of the personal characteristics
[b]elow **BEST DESCRIBES** what you **MOST DISLIKE**
[a]bout Gary Hart?

[H]e does not care enough about people's
   problems. . . . . ☐ G(1)
[H]e's not a strong leader . . . . . . ☐ (2)
[H]is ideas are out of date. . . . . . ☐ (3)
[H]e's tied to special interests . . . ☐ (4)
[H]e'd bring changes that would hurt
   the poor. . . . . ☐ (5)
[H]e's unclear about what he stands for ☐ (6)
[H]e may not always be honest. . . . . ☐ (7)
[H]e pays too much attention to his
   style and image . . . . ☐ (8)

[.] Which **ONE** of the personal characteristics
[b]elow **BEST DESCRIBES** what you **MOST DISLIKE**
[a]bout Walter Mondale?

[H]e does not care enough about people's
   problems. . . . . ☐ H(1)
[H]e's not a strong leader . . . . . . ☐ (2)
[H]is ideas are out of date. . . . . . ☐ (3)
[H]e's tied to special interests . . . ☐ (4)
[H]e'd bring changes that would hurt
   the poor. . . . . ☐ (5)
[H]e's unclear about what he stands for ☐ (6)
[H]e may not always be honest. . . . . ☐ (7)
[H]e pays too much attention to his
   style and image . . . . ☐ (8)

[.] Which **ONE** of the statements below **BEST
D**[E]SCRIBES why you voted for the candidate of
[y]our choice in the presidential primary today?

[H]e'd handle foreign affairs well . . ☐ I(1)
[H]e'd produce a strong economy. . . . ☐ (2)
[H]e'd hold down unemployment. . . . . ☐ (3)
[H]e'd reduce the federal deficit. . . ☐ (4)
[H]e'd hold down government spending . ☐ (5)
[H]e'd keep us out of war . . . . . . ☐ (6)
[H]e'd deal well with the problems of
   the poor and the elderly . . . . ☐ (7)

(OVER)

This year, for the first time, ABC is trying to determine if the time of day people vote has any effect on *how* they vote. CBS has polled voters about this, and has discovered that conservatives tend to vote early and that more liberal blue-collar workers vote late. Jeffrey Alderman, the head of ABC's polling division, says he is going ahead with his own research because of technical problems he perceives in his competitor's methodology. Such distrust is routine among the players of the polling game. They even *lie* to one another. Alderman recalls a phone call he received shortly before the primary season got under way. "A guy from CBS I knew a bit asked, 'How many states are you doing?' I lied to him. But I think he knew it was a lie."

Questions aimed at discovering why voters cast their ballots for a particular candidate are crucial for print-media pundits. Americans almost always know the winners and losers before they go to bed on election night; what they want from their morning papers is an explanation of the outcome. What newspaper people want and get from ABC is primary-night access to the information turned up by the "why" questions. Pollsters say that these questions must be multiple-choice and must not burden the respondent with too many possible answers. (Speed is crucial in exit polling—voters simply will not spend much time filling out a form.) The decisions about which issues to raise in question 8 and about the wording of the answers were worked out by ABC's news division. According to Alderman, the first step in formulating possible answers to this question was a phone survey, in which potential voters were asked open-ended questions like "What is the biggest problem facing our nation today?" Given that there are only seven possible answers, question 8 effectively delegitimizes issues—why no mention of tax reform, or of *military* spending? Since analysts and commentators base their explanations of election results on the answers to questions like this, exit polling ultimately narrows the political discourse. Bill Kovach, the Washington bureau chief of the *New York Times*, wonders "if the media and the polls are feeding on each other. Is there a danger that other ideas, other issues or approaches, are being squeezed out and an incomplete agenda is being drawn?"

Question 10, like many others on the ballot, does not allow the respondent to answer "None of the above." Can this throw off a survey? Many experts say yes: individuals will sometimes check *any* box rather than appear ignorant. Thirty-five years ago, students at eight universities checked off the nonexistent "Danireans" as people they found unacceptable as marriage partners for their relatives. Recently, pollsters for the West German newsweekly *Der Spiegel* asked readers to arrange a list of cabinet members in order of popularity. A fictitious minister came in sixth, ahead of ten others.

Number 11 is for so-called grab-bag questions. For example, a question of local interest might be asked. In the New York Democratic primary exit poll there was a question on the importance of New York City Mayor Ed Koch's and Governor Mario Cuomo's endorsements of Walter Mondale. But not just any topic makes it into number 11. Early in the Democratic primary, some ABC staff members lobbied hard for a question about the impact of the movie *The Right Stuff*. Pollster Alderman fought them off. "I knew from the numbers on movie ticket sales that no one was seeing the picture," he said. Note the blank space next to box 5: if a late-breaking development is deemed important to the campaign, a question about it can be included at the last minute. Through April, ABC had yet to find a topic hot enough to fill the space.

Before the New Hampshire primary, ABC pollsters drew up a poll to be taken every few days during the two weeks leading up to primary day. Politicians have used such surveys for years, but this was the first time a network conducted a "tracking" poll. It was a smash hit: ABC caught the swelling wave for Gary Hart rumbling east from Iowa. Some critics of tracking polls say that the changes in voters' preferences recorded every seventy-two hours or so are just swings within a poll's margin of error—phony volatility. Alderman believes that the whimsy and indecision and last-minute stampedes are real, and he planted question 13 in the exit poll to prove it. He says the results bear him out: in New Hampshire, for example, 23 percent of those polled in the primary said they made up their minds on the day of or the day prior to the vote.

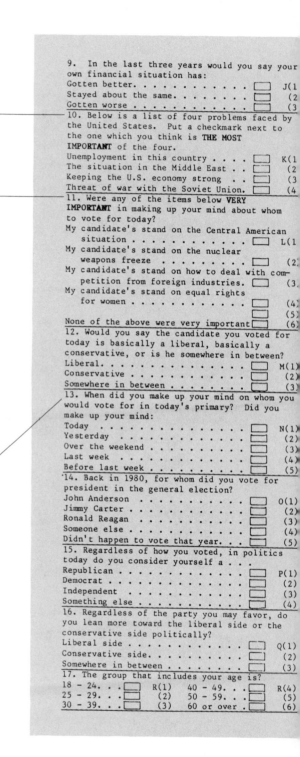

What's your religious preference?

otestant	☐	S(1)
tholic	☐	(2)
wish	☐	(3)
me other religion.	☐	(4)
religion	☐	(5)

Does the chief wage earner in your ─── usehold get paid an hourly rate, paid a lary or is the chief wage earner lf-employed? (IF CHIEF WAGE EARNER IS TIRED, CHECK THE BOX THAT BEST DESCRIBES HOW E CHIEF WAGE EARNER USED TO BE PAID AND ECK THE "RETIRED" BOX AS WELL.)

urly . . .	☐ T(1)	Retired now. ☐	(5)
lary . . .	☐ (2)		
lf-employed	☐ (3)		
employed .	☐ (4)		

Which one of the categories below best scribes most of your ancestors? (CHECK ONE LY)

rman or Austrian	☐	U(1)
nnsylvania Dutch	☐	(2)
glish, Scottish or Welsh	☐	(3)
ish.	☐	(4)
lish/other Slavic.	☐	(5)
alian.	☐	(6)
spanic	☐	(7)
ro-American.	☐	(8)
mething else (WRITE IN BELOW). . .	☐	(9)

Are you or anyone in your household a ion member?

s. . . . . ☐ V(1)	No. . . . . ☐	(2)

What was the last grade of school you mpleted?

me high school or less	☐	W(1)
gh school graduate	☐	(2)
me college	☐	(3)
llege graduate	☐	(4)
stgraduate	☐	(5)

Your sex is:

le . . . . ☐ X(1)	Female. . . ☐	(2)

Are you Black, White or some other race?

ack	☐	Y(1)
ite	☐	(2)
me other race.	☐	(3)

Into which group below does your annual usehold income before taxes fall?

der $5,000	☐	Z(1)
,000 to $9,999	☐	(2)
0,000 to $19,999	☐	(3)
0,000 to $29,999	☐	(4)
0,000 to $39,999	☐	(5)
0,000 to $49,999	☐	(6)
0,000 and over	☐	(7)

EASE FOLD IN HALF AND PLACE IN "SECRET ─── LLOT" BOX. THANK YOU FOR YOUR COOPERATION.

No one at ABC is proud of question 19. Designed to get a read on the voting patterns of retired blue-collar workers, it managed only to confuse retirees of all stripes. Many checked off the box designating "retired now" but ignored those pertaining to method of pay. Questions often flop the first time around. Says William Schneider, a resident fellow at the American Enterprise Institute and a polling consultant to the *Los Angeles Times*: "People tend to forget that polling remains more an art than a science."

The networks start looking at completed exit polls around 1 P.M. Pollsters usually have some indication of the outcome of an election by early evening. When they should begin *revealing* this information is the issue. In 1980, on the basis of exit polls and returns from sample precincts, Ronald Reagan's victory was announced ("projected") by the networks before the polls had closed in some parts of the country. Do early projections discourage people who haven't voted from doing so? John E. Jackson, a political scientist at the University of Michigan, has done the most sophisticated study of early returns, and he says yes. Jackson has concluded that among registered voters who had not gone to the polls by 6 P.M. (EST), learning of Reagan's "victory" lowered the probability that they would vote by 6 percentage points in the East, 9 percentage points in the South, and 12 percentage points in the Midwest and West. A solution? Washington and Wyoming passed laws last year banning exit polling within 300 feet of the polls, a strong deterrent. The three major networks and the *New York Times* have gone to federal court to fight the Washington law. Albert Cantril, director of the Bureau of Social Science Research in Washington, D.C., has proposed a no-first-use doctrine of sorts: until the effects of exit polls are firmly established, networks should not make projections based on them. ABC's Alderman is not impressed by Cantril's proposal. "That man," he says, "must be living in a monastery."

Clock on bureau reads 11:12 as I start timed experiment to test theory by painter and photocollagist David Hockney. Talking in the *New Yorker* last summer about "ordinary" photography as a "medium for the artist," he said his "main argument was that a photograph could not be looked at for a long time. . . . You can't look at most photographs for more than, say, thirty seconds. It has nothing to do with the subject matter. . . . I mean, photography is all right if you don't mind looking at the world from the point of view of a paralyzed cyclops—*for a split second*. But that's not what it's like to live in the world. . . . At a museum, you can easily spend half an hour looking at a Canaletto and you won't blank out. . . . And the reason you can't look at a photograph for a long time is because there's virtually no time *in it*. . . ." Ordinary photograph, by James Hamilton. Unusual clock. (Elapsed viewing time: 1 sec.)

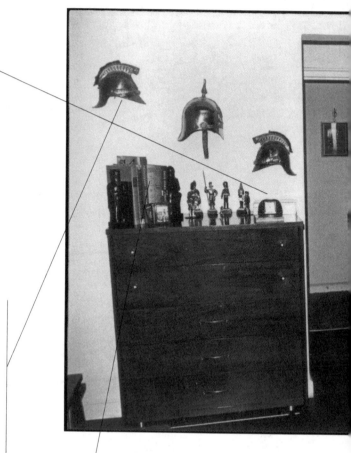

What the—?! Instinctive glance at woman is diverted by diagonal of big shiny helmets. Attached to wall? How? Or hung from ceiling by fishing line? While woman's form, muffled in busy housecoat, is located in real space by perspective of hallway, helmets' polished surfaces and classically graceful outlines float against flat area, abstracted: weirdly hovering. Are these all really in same space and time implied by informal tilt of wide-angle framing and homely details (Kleenex holder behind clock, metal strip along wall-to-wall hall rug, woman's scuffs, etc.)? Only natural for my eye to insinuate helmets into context by looking for human head to fit one on. Sole available head, woman's, already wearing one: hairdo shaped like helmet nearest her. (Elapsed time: 9 min.)

Way over Hockney's 30-sec. limit already. Rotate photo 90 degrees to read book titles: *Thus Spake Zarathustra*, Aeschylus' *The Ore-----*, *Rights of Man*. Rights of man pretty well defended here! And not just by looming specter of three Roman legionnaires. Note pair of sinister phallic-Africana bookend sentries; six guardsmen (all the more spikily belligerent in sharp-focus miniature); and, far to the right, mobilized ranks of rough-hewn chessmen (in suitably gothic shadow, fresh from forest combat in animated horror movie by Ingmar Bergman). (23 min.)

Veronica Geng is the author of Partners *and* Love Trouble Is My Business, *both published by Harper & Row. She is on the staff of* The New Yorker.

YOU BLANK OUT?

theory, *by Veronica Geng*

Dogs in painting patrol their side of doorway, ready to scent intruders. This a Canaletto? Unlikely he dabbled in English-hunt genre. Try to muse on it as forged Canaletto, but blank out. Still under Hockney's ½-hr. Canaletto time. (29 min., 59 sec.)

Liquor bottles make me laugh. Why? Am I losing touch with "what it's like to live in the world"? OK by me. In "the world," joke could be that bar cart is in ridiculous taste. Hamilton's photo rigorously prevents this loaded subject matter from slopping over into snide social comment, or maudlin portraiture, by steering my attention back and forth among visual facts. All those soldierly verticals suddenly take in bottles and glasses, too, transforming them into a rattling militia. In flanking position, tubby ice bucket and pitcher have spit-and-polish style of Tweedledum and Tweedledee dressed for a nice battle in pots and pans. Split second of film exposure time may have "paralyzed" rolling bar cart, but as imagery it has a fantastical spin. May be even more mobile in photo than in reality: just when *was* the last time it was moved? How recently was stoppered decanter used? (These always look as if nobody remembers what the stuff in them is.) Where is man who usually presides over bar? Room is obviously his den, defended at all vantage points by dogs and soldiers. (3/4 hr.)

Until now, it was *too soon* to look at the woman. (Photo has enforced a kind of tact. In "the world" it's rude to inspect the decor while ignoring the hostess, but photo says it's proper to let time inform one's view of people.) She's defined by analogies to husband's den: helmeted, aggressively patterned, relaxed yet watchfully on duty (in housecoat, but fully made-up; one hand easily in pocket, the other holding cigarette angled like lance of toy Swiss guard). Dogs and soldiers are only inanimate metaphors for her. Blocking the door, she's really the one holding the fort.

In the *Odyssey*, Odysseus' wife, Penelope, playing for time until his homecoming, tolerated in their household 108 suitors clamoring for her presumably widowed hand. While the warrior-goddess Athena urged that they be killed for their abuse of hospitality, they hung around drinking up Odysseus' wine. No such guests could worm their way in here. This wife, her husband absent, guards his liquor—his little army of liquid courage. With helmet and lance, attributes of Athena, this modern Penelope turns patience into vigilance. Clock still says 11:12. (Total elapsed time: approx. 3,000 yrs.)

Last June, S_____ was graduated from a public high school in suburban Connecticut, one regarded as among America's finest. For the purpose of getting into a good college, the quality and reputation of a high school are as important as how well a student does. Doing moderately well at a mediocre school is no compelling achievement. This transcript, once its numbers and signs and shorthand, reveals a good deal about this student, about this school—and, unwittingly, about what passes for an adequate education.

Ceramics and sculpture, photography, theater, and chorus—all such worthy but marginal subjects suggest, if not the intellectual character of a school, at least its affluence. Critics argue that public high schools waste student's time with trivial classes and non-essential activities; this transcript seems to support the contention. S_____'s school day should have been take up with four or five demanding courses. Instead, various electives, offered in the name of personal growth, crowd the day. S struggled in the art courses (Cs), and had the good sense to flunk "Clothing."

S_____ took one year of U.S. history as a sophomore. She also studied modern European history as well as India and Southeast Asia, albeit for half a year each. This is the entire classroom source for her historical perspective.

S_____ had two years of biology and one of chemistry. She apparently was not willing (or able) to avoid laboratory science. Yet she never studied physics. And although the school made sure she took some of the old and proper studies in mathematics—algebra, geometry, perhaps pre-calculus in "Functions"—she presumable has no experience with probability or statistics. It cannot be assured that she has attained mathematical literacy.

Leon Botstein is president of Bard College and of Simon's Rock College and professor of music and history at Bard College.

SECONDARY SCHOOL R

STUDENT IN

| Last Name | First Name | Middle Name |

| Home Address | City | State | Zip |

Parent or Guardian

Previous Secondary School Attended (if any)   Date

GRADE	SUBJECTS	LEVEL	SPECIAL NOTE	FINAL GRADE	CRED
				C	02
09	CER + SCULP			C	02
09	LIN + WOOD CUTS			B	1
09	ENGLISH 9-2			B	1
09	FRENCH B			C+	
09	FRENCH 9 USERS			C	
09	BASIC FOODS			A	0
09	CHILD DEVELOP			F	
09	CLOTHING			C	
09	ALGEBRA I			C	0
09	CHORUS 9			C+	0
09	P.E 9			C+	
09	EARTH SCI			B	
09	SOC STU 9			B	
10	SOPHOMORE PE			A-	
10	SOPHOMORE PE			B+	
10	SOPHOMORE PE			A-	
10	SOPHOMORE PE			B+	
10	DRIVERS ED			A-	
10	DRAMA 1			B+	
10	SOPHOMORE CHORS			B+	
10	ENGLISH 2A			C+	
10	FRENCH 3 USERS	A		B-	
10	GEOMETRY B	A	LAB	B-	
10	BIOLOGY 1	A		B-	
10	US TO 1898	A		B-	
10	US SINCE 1898	A		F	
11	IND ST PHYS ED				
11	THEATRE 2			B+	
11	BASIC PHOTOGRAP			B+	
11	WOMNS GLEE CLUB			B+	
11	ENGLISH 3A	A		C+	
11	FRENCH 4 SPKRS	B		B-	
11	ALGEBRA 2B	A	LAB	C+	
11	CHEM 1 SURVEY	A		B-	
11	MOD EUR HISTORY	A		B	
11	PSYCHOLOGY	A			

SENIOR CLASSES

12	THEATER 3				
12	CP TYPING			A	
12	CREAT WRIT SEM			A	
12	AP ENGLISH	AP		A	
12	FRENCH 5 SPKRS	A		A	
12	FRENCH 5 SPKRS	A		A	
12	FRNCH ADV RDNGS	A		A	
12	FUNCTIONS P	B		B	
12	BIOLOGY 2	A	LAB	A	
12	INDIA/SE ASIA	A		A	

EARNED SO FAR

ollege, by Leon Botstein

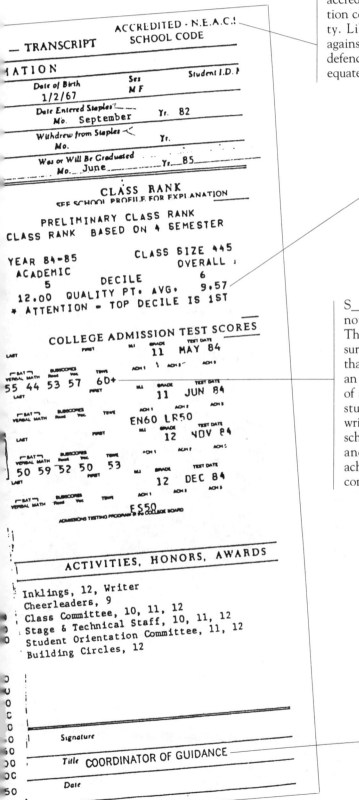

The school, which has some 2,000 students, is accredited by a regional association. Such accreditation constitutes a feeble assurance of academic quality. Like state regulations, accreditation protects against only the most flagrant deficiencies. It is no defence against bad teaching, poor curricula, or inadequate facilities.

The overall grade-point average is made up of all courses except gym. Chorus taken for credit, in other words, is weighted on the same basis as English. This high school shows its concern for its image as a competitive institution by also calculating an "academic average"; not all schools bother to make the pretense.

S_____'s scores on the Scholastic Aptitude Test are not spectacular, although they are above average. The subscores for verbal (graded from 20 to 80) measure reading and vocabulary skills; experience shows that above-average scores like these do not indicate an ability to read critically or write clearly. The "test of standard English" (TSWE) merely requires that a student "recognize" standard written English, not write it. Although S_____ has done passably well in school, has once gotten the top score on the TSWE, and has taken advanced placement courses and achievement tests in English, she may not be able to compose a straightforward, analytical argument.

The guidance "coordinator" (he most likely does not know S_____ well) signs the transcript and mails it off, knowing she will be admitted to one of the many reasonably competitive colleges in America. Yet it is likely that S_____ does not know what is in the Constitution; knows nothing about economics; can tell you little about the theory and practice of capitalism, socialism, or communism; cannot grasp the science and technology germane to medicine or defense; has never read *The Republic*, the *Koran*, or *The Brothers Karamazov*. It is also reasonable to assume that hers has been a passive education by textbooks, workbooks, and multiple choice tests, in oversize classes and from teachers better versed in pedagogy than in their respective disciplines. And this is one of the country's best high schools.

This photograph, taken in 1978 at a lodge in Poland's Lake District, shows a group of staff members and friends (and a few guards at the lodge) celebrating the twentieth year of the journal *Polityka* under the direction of its chief editor, Mieczyslaw Rakowski. In the 1970s, *Polityka* was the foremost liberal weekly in Eastern Europe, projecting a pragmatic, technocratic, cautiously reformist line—sort of a Polish version of the current *New Republic*. But the ensuing years—with the upsurge of Solidarity and then its suppression by martial law four years ago this month—tore the fabric of this happy scene. Poland's journalists were to play an especially important role during these years: some of those pictured here ended up as well-paid government officials, others as leading (unemployed) oppositionists. Thus, the photograph contains a hidden parable: the pressures of history can force liberals to show their true faces, to live out their moral and political world views.

Mieczyslaw Rakowski, the son of peasants, is in many ways a consummate son of Communist Poland. Few have proved so masterful at the country's slippery games of power. Rakowski rose to the helm of *Polityka* in 1958 and steered a modestly adventuresome course thereafter—reformist, but never *too*. He always supported his patrons in the party leadership until just before any shuffle, at which point he'd stake out a "reformist" position favoring their ouster. (His supple opportunism was cleverly documented in Leopold Tyrmand's celebrated essay "The Hair-Styles of M. Rakowski.") As late as July 1980 he was still championing the corrupt regime of Edward Gierek, but by early September, following the strike in Gdansk, he had, true to form, discovered the desperate need for institutional "credibility." Gierek soon fell. In February 1981, the day General Wojciech Jaruzelski was appointed prime minister, Rakowski was named deputy prime minister in charge of negotiations with Solidarity. In this capacity, he always tried to portray himself as "the good cop," protecting the union from the far meaner designs of "the bad cops"—but the concessions he demanded were identical. Although he'd long claimed to favor "partnership" with Solidarity, he helped supervise the December 13, 1981, martial-law coup and with it the jailing of his one-time negotiating partners. He told a gathering of party functionaries a few days later, "The horse which is galloping wildly must be brought back to a trot. . . . [I]t has to *obey*."

Ryszard Kapuściński, Poland's foremost international correspondent, spent the 1970s publishing a series of reportages on the corruption and downfall of foreign tyrants—Haile Selassie in Ethiopia, the Shah in Iran. These pieces offered barely veiled allegories of the situation in Poland, but the censors felt compelled to let them through for fear of admitting the resemblances. Since the coup, he has refused to publish in the official media; he is currently writing on the military regime of Uganda's Idi Amin.

FROM FOKSAL '81, BY DARIUSZ FIKUS. ANEKS/LONDON.

AND BRIGHTEST

...ocus, by Lawrence Weschler

Wieslaw Gornicki, a longtime foreign correspondent based for many years in the United States (where he was known for his hobby of collecting toy soldiers), spent much of 1980–81 back in Poland criticizing the pro-Solidarity tendencies of the Journalists Association. Even so, many were surprised to discover him on their TVs in the days immediately following the December 1981 coup, trussed up *in a military uniform*—the official spokesman for the generals' junta. In recognition of his good works, he was rapidly promoted from captain to major.

Hanna Krall, who won fame for her deeply empathetic interviews, remained on the *Polityka* staff throughout the Solidarity period, using the venue to publish ever more daring interviews with figures from earlier Polish uprisings. Her interview with Anna Walentynowicz, the beloved Gdansk activist, is a seminal document of the Solidarity period. Following the coup, Krall quit *Polityka* and political journalism altogether. She is now writing autobiographical fiction, which she only publishes abroad.

Jerzy Urban, formerly *Polityka*'s national editor, is currently the government's chief press spokesman. His regularly scheduled news conferences feature ostentatiously cynical displays of power. When asked about Western trade sanctions, shortly after the coup, he pointed out that "the authorities will always eat their fill." He seems particularly to savor dismissing all questions about Solidarity with such locutions as "The government takes a stand only on important issues, and this is of no significance whatsoever." In March 1984, however, Urban's daughter married a Solidarity activist, and the wedding announcements were printed and distributed by NOWA, Poland's leading underground publishing house.

Dariusz Fikus took a leave from his job as *Polityka*'s managing editor in 1980 to assume the openly elected position of secretary general of the Journalists Association. Like many of the journalists pictured here, Fikus quit *Polityka* right after the coup. (The journal itself plods on, carefully toeing the line.) He became managing editor of *The Blind Cooperativist*, a once innocuous magazine for the blind which suddenly became quite topical and much sought-after. He also composed *Foksal '81*, a memoir which he published by way of the underground. In that book, he recounts the story of his last meeting with Rakowski. Fikus went to the deputy prime minister's office in December 1981 to deliver his resignation from *Polityka*. Rakowski urged him to reconsider. At one point the conversation was interrupted by an urgent phone call from Wroclaw, where, it seems, students were holding a candlelight vigil at a dorm. Rakowski ordered the students flushed out of the dorm and their leaders expelled, hung up the phone, and then, without missing a beat, resumed his conversation with Fikus, extolling the virtues of patient liberalism.

Lawrence Weschler is a staff writer at The New Yorker, *covering Poland for the past decade. He is the author of* The Passion of Poland *and* A Miracle, a Universe: Settling Accounts with Torturers.

FILLING OUT T

The bureaucrat at death

Last year in the United States 2,127,000 deaths were reported on a form such as this. The U.S. Standard Certificate of Death, in use since 1900, combines the objectifying tendency of modern medicine with the bureaucratic imperative to collect, classify, and record. Data compiled from the certificates are used to calculate national death rates for diseases as well as to rank the causes of death, and thus set priorities for the allocation of health funds. Ultimately, the "rank" of a disease determines which lives the goverment deems worth saving.

Prior to this century, deaths were tallied by burial counts rather than certificates. The rise of professional medicine—combined with the predisposition of Protestants during the Second Great Awakening to view disease in moral terms—encouraged the shift to certificates. "By demonstrating the existence of evils," Quaker physician Gouverneur Emerson wrote, "statistics may lead to a removal of their causes." In 1847, at the founding convention of the American Medical Association, Emerson joined with the president of the American Statistical Association, Lemuel Shattuck, in calling for a standard death certificate. Subsequent legislation removed registration from the hands of church sextons and cemetery caretakers and placed it within the purview of licensed physicians. Yet current medical practice seems encumbered by nineteenth-century attitudes regarding the causes of disease.

When Liberace's doctor listed subacute encephalopathy, a brain disease, as the entertainer's cause of death, he claimed to be acting to the best of his knowledge. But coroner Raymond Carrillo, citing autopsy findings of a form of pneumonia typically found in patients whose immune systems are crippled by AIDS, refused to accept the certificate; he maintained that Liberace's physician had known all along that he had AIDS. We use mortality data to rivet attention on diseases, such as cancer, that strike without deference to one's station or wealth. But moral judgments are never far from the surface.

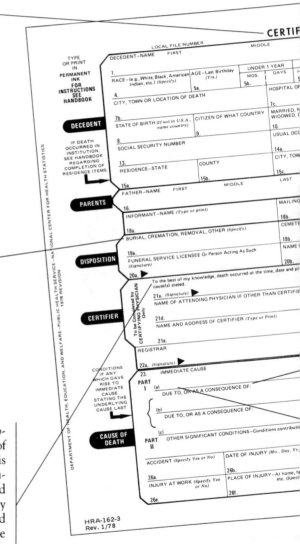

Michael Zimecki is a medical writer for the University of Pittsburgh Medical Center, His wife, Helen, died from complications of diabetes.

HE LAST FORM

oor, *by Michael Zimecki*

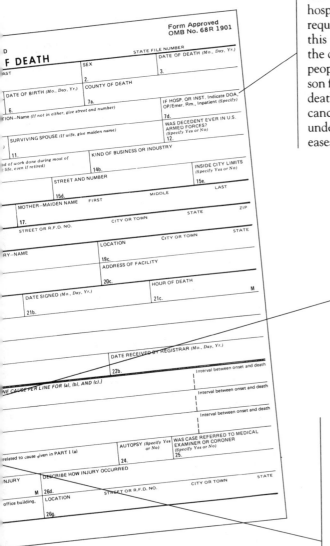

Before 1940, deaths were recorded by place of occurrence rather than actual residence. As a result, death rates tended to be inflated for locations with major hospitals, rest homes, sanitoriums, etc. Current rules requiring completion of the residence line eliminate this bias; however, place of death continues to skew the data in another important way. Today, since most people die in hospitals rather than at home, the reason for admission is often listed as the primary cause of death—this practice tends to exaggerate the significance of acute conditions, such as heart failure, and underestimates the role of chronic, degenerative diseases, such as diabetes.

The last condition listed here is considered to be the primary cause of death; it is used to calculate national death rates. The certifier must reconstruct the sequence of events leading to death, a process subject to judgmental error. AIDS, for example, is a narrowly defined disease, indicated by the presence of *Pneumocystis carinii* pneumonia, Kaposi's sarcoma, and other lymphomas, but its possible manifestations can also include non-specific pneumonias, tuberculosis, and heart disease. Professional unwillingness to adopt a broader definition of AIDS contributes to serious under-reporting of deaths from this disease. Officially, 39,060 people have died from AIDS since 1981, but authorities concede that the actual number is closer to 43,000. Unofficial estimates are even higher.

Mortality statistics also underestimate the severity of other diseases, such as diabetes, that are more common among the poor, non-whites, and women. It is estimated that diabetes is listed on less than half the death certificates of people with the disease: when diabetes does appear, three quarters of the time it is listed only as a contributing cause. These deaths are not reflected in national rankings. It is difficult to say how many of these "missing" deaths involve conditions, such as stroke or renal disease, that are clearly associated with or even caused by diabetes, but the number could range up to 170,000 annually. The U.S. Standard Certificate of Death is our last offering to a bureaucracy that reduces lives to numbers. It records our final day and hour (permanent ink, of course), but statistics based upon it are neither as indelible nor as certain as they appear.